PENGUIN

Handbag Heaven

Maggie Alderson was born in London, brought up in Staffordshire, and educated at the University of St Andrews. She has worked on nine glossy magazines – as editor on four of them – and two newspapers. As well as her column, 'Style Notes', for *Good Weekend*, she contributes to leading newspapers and magazines in Britain and the US. Her first book, *Shoe Money*, was published in 1998 and her bestselling novel, *Pants on Fire*, in 2000. She is currently at work on her second novel.

IN PRAISE OF *SHOE MONEY*

Maggie Alderson undercuts her fashion addiction
with sly wit and bracing good sense.

Helen Garner

If you're in the mood for something short, cute and fluffy,
this will look gorgeous on you.

The Age

It's only fair to warn you: this book is wickedly funny.
Not sly smile or knowing grin funny, but public menace,
weep with laughter, embarrass yourself on buses funny . . .
Buy several copies and give them to your favourite female friends.
But read it on the bus at your peril.

Sydney Morning Herald

Compulsory reading for any girl who'd rather buy a new pair of
shoes than a toaster, hates shopping for swimsuits, and wears far
too much black. Alderson's book – which is a collection of her
regular newspaper columns – makes hilarious reading.

Cosmopolitan

A firm follower of the does-it-make-my-bum-look-big? school of shopping, Alderson toddles you along past perfect handbags, pondering that nothing seems as faultless as something you wore and loved when young, and asking, 'Where are the flattering mirrors, please?' . . . Fortunately, although she knows the address of Frock-Heaven, a what's-all-this-then? attitude and a pair of large pearl earrings makes it all endurable – like a good talk on the telephone with someone funny.

Harper's Bazaar & Mode

Alderson has plenty to say and a handbag (preferably Hermès) full of jokes and one-liners. If you love fashion but baulk at the pretentiousness that can surround it, then *Shoe Money* is the book for you.

Cleo

The editor of this magazine laughed so much when reading Maggie Alderson's new book while on an interstate flight, that the man in the next seat leaned over and begged to know its name. *Shoe Money* will have every female reader laughing and saying 'Yes!', and every male reader laughing and learning a lot.

Australian Gourmet Traveller

Maggie Alderson

Handbag Heaven

with illustrations by the author

PENGUIN BOOKS

Penguin Books Australia Ltd
487 Maroondah Highway, PO Box 257
Ringwood, Victoria 3134, Australia
Penguin Books Ltd
Harmondsworth, Middlesex, England
Penguin Putnam Inc.
375 Hudson Street, New York, New York 10014, USA
Penguin Books Canada Limited
10 Alcorn Avenue, Toronto, Ontario, Canada M4V 3B2
Penguin Books (NZ) Ltd
Cnr Rosedale and Airborne Roads, Albany, Auckland, New Zealand
Penguin Books (South Africa) (Pty) Ltd
24 Sturdee Avenue, Rosebank, Johannesburg 2196, South Africa
Penguin Books India (P) Ltd
11, Community Centre, Panchsheel Park, New Delhi 110 017, India

First published by Penguin Books Australia 2001

1 3 5 7 9 10 8 6 4 2

Front cover photography by Tim De Neefe, bag by Jamin Puech.
Back cover photography by Jennifer Soo and Tim De Neefe, middle bag by Jamin
Puech, bags to left and right by Fendi.
Designed by Debra Billson, Penguin Design Studio
Typeset in 11.5/17 Bembo by Post Pre-Press Group, Brisbane, Queensland
Printed and bound in Australia by McPherson's Printing Group, Maryborough, Victoria

National Library of Australia
Cataloguing-in-Publication data:

Alderson, Maggie.
Handbag Heaven

ISBN 0 14 300005 5.
1. Lifestyles – Australia. 2. Fashion – Australia. I. Title.

070.444

www.penguin.com.au

For Mary

Contents

The divine Miss N

'I also have Rita Hayworth's nightdress . . .' What do you say to a remark like that? I just nodded. Sitting next to Naomi Campbell on a small sofa, I could barely speak anyway, I was so in awe of her beauty. Okay, she looks pretty good in pictures, does our Nomes, and I've seen her strutting along catwalks about a million times, but nothing prepares you for her at close hand. Her eyes could silence a multitude. Her profile could cause earthquakes. Her slightest smile could melt a glacier. And she had the most fabulous pair of shoes on . . .

'I'm wearing Gucci today,' she said, looking down at her tottering-heeled, brown kid court shoes and waggling her ankles like a three-year-old with new sandals. 'I have loads of shoes, because at the end of a show if you say, "Like these shoes", they say, "Take 'em", and you walk out

1

with a bag full. I normally wear Manolos.'

Well, why wouldn't you? If Mr Blahnik were pressing them upon you at every turn and the nearest you ever got to public transport was a stretch limo, why wouldn't you wear Manolos every day? And if I were Naomi Campbell, I'd collect Hermès Kelly bags, too.

'I like Jamin Puech bags,' she said, with all the grace of Martina Hingis saying she enjoyed the odd game of ping-pong. 'They're really cute, but you can't fit much in them.'

And she certainly seems to carry a lot around with her. At her feet was a huge, baby blue Hermès Birkin bag, which weighed a tonne when she let me pet it on my lap for a moment. Can't imagine what she keeps in it, apart from her Nokia mobile phone, which she whipped out to show me like the good little spokesmodel that she is.

'It's like a lipstick,' she said, flipping it open and reeling off its technical attributes. Ker-ching, Naomi earned her fee. Great. With that over we could get on to more stuff about handbags and shoes.

'I love Fendi bags. I've got my favourite baguette next door. Wanna see?' Too bloody right. A flunky brought it in. I stroked it. 'I collect old Kellys,' she continued, meaning the handbags, not elderly Irish people. 'I've got one from the 1920s which is grey leather with platinum fittings. I got it at Didier Ludot's shop in the Palais Royal in Paris.' I nodded furiously. I bought a handbag there myself once.

2

We were practically related.

'I collect vintage clothes, too,' she said. 'There's a shop in LA called Rita & Lily where I got a leopard-skin coat and turban. I wore the coat in Paris once and a sixty-nine-year-old couturier at Dior said, "That's my coat. I made it. Do you know who that belonged to?" Then he showed me the name inside – Ann-Margret.'

And talking about all that led on to the remark about Rita Hayworth's nightie, as well as details of a red Balenciaga dress that Audrey Hepburn wore in *Funny Face*.

And it's not just vintage dresses of impeccable provenance that fill Naomi's closets: 'I have dresses from Versace and Alaïa and YSL and Chanel which are unique. They have to be numbered and catalogued in case they ever want them for a museum.'

Crikey. But with such riches to choose from, how does she decide what to wear every morning? 'I walk around in nothing, saying, "What will I wear?" It might be anything from a sari to a hippie look. Anything I feel comfortable in. I don't like looking like other people.'

That, my dear, is never going to be a problem.

P.S. After the interview, Naomi sent me a personal card to thank me. Her name was printed on it in pink ink and the envelope was lined with pink tissue. We are definitely related.

3

Just desserts

Somebody recently asked me the oblique question, 'What is your fashion mantra?' I realise now she was actually asking me for predigested 'fashion tips' along the lines of 'Never wear a G-string under tight white pants', or 'Try not to weigh more than your IQ', but at the time I thought she meant a small phrase that you repeat over and over again in your head when meditating on fashion.

Either way, I have since worked out what my fashion mantra is. It's 'If I just . . .' It must be, because that's what I repeat to myself endlessly when contemplating the great unanswerable 'om' of my wardrobe.

'If I just . . . If I just . . . If I just had a Helmut Lang suit, I would always have something to wear to work and then out to glamour cocktails without changing. If I just had a black Longchamp tote, I would have room for all my workday junk, without looking like a nomad. If I just found the right pair of shoes, I'd be able to stride around all day in comfort without feeling like a Teletubby. If I just lost five kilos, everything really nice in my wardrobe would fit me again.'

But it's becoming clear to me that there is something fundamentally wrong with my fashion mantra, because far from bringing me peace, non-attachment and general sartorial nirvana, it has become a self-perpetuating cycle of unfulfillable desire.

Take Jamin Puech bags. For nearly a year my chant was, 'If I just . . . If I just . . . If I just had a Jamin Puech bag, it wouldn't matter what else I wore, because the bag would be so unique and special and characterful.'

For so long I resisted this urge to spend an unjustifiably large sum of money on an impractically small handbag. I was steely in my determination, even when I was staying in a Paris hotel right opposite a boutique which had the perfect little beaded baglet hanging in the window. I fingered them in Paddington, I stroked them in London, I patted them in Milan, but still I didn't give in to temptation. Until New Year's Eve 1999, when it seemed likely the world was going to end at midnight anyway and I thought I might as well go with a Jamin Puech in my hand.

For a few weeks my life did feel complete. I swung that little bag around like an altar boy with a censer, gathering compliments with the same ease as I attract pet hairs, and then I went back to the European fashion shows in March. All the little beaded bags had gone. Even the girl from US *Vogue* who had impressed me so much last time by carrying two Jamin Puechs every day (she couldn't fit her stuff into one she told me, so she carried two) was now carrying a Louis Vuitton monogrammed bag. (I think it was a Trocadero, but I'm still learning the names.)

Now I have the perfect little evening bag and the perfect in-flight bag ('If I just had a Prada messenger bag . . .'), but my life is still incomplete because I don't have the perfect chic workday bag. So when I give in to temptation, as I inevitably will, what 'If I just . . .' will it be after that? Whatever Louis Vuitton, Tod's, Fendi and all the rest of them decide to serve up. You'd think I'd know by now that the whole point of fashion is to make you feel you don't just want stuff – you 'need' it. The day just one more thing does make my life complete is the day Miuccia Prada goes out of business.

With that new wisdom, I think I'd better change my mantra to a contemplation of the words of someone who really knew a thing or two about meditation – Mr Buddha. 'The root of all suffering is desire,' he said. And judging by that remark, you'd think he knew something about fashion, too.

Size matters

What dress size are you? I'm a size 4. Well, that's what it says on the label of my Donna Karan jacket, so I must be. But on my Zimmermann dress it says 14.

I've got Collette Dinnigan garments in small, medium and large. My jeans are 30, my agnès b. skirts are 38 and my Giorgio Armani jacket is 44. I'm a size 10 trouser at David Lawrence, but a size 12 jacket. My Easton Pearson new best dress is a 10, but I can't even fit into a size 14 in Scanlan & Theodore.

So what size am I really? Damned if I know.

It's not just a matter of my ever-changing waistline. This does demand a certain range of size options across the wardrobe, but they are generally provided for by switching to all-jersey clothes and elastic waistbands for the two months after I have done my *Sydney Morning Herald*

Good Food Guide reviews and gained about six kilos, until the Liver Cleansing Diet works its magic again.

Sometimes I'll wear the size 4 jacket and the size 14 dress on the same day and they'll both appear to fit correctly. Even I can't put on six kilos between lunch and dinner. So what gives with this sizing malarky? Of course, overseas sizing systems add hugely to the confusion. I have here a conversion chart which came with my new Hanro knickers (they're Swiss, which explains why they're so multi-lingual). It's like a phrase book for the international language of dress sizes ('Hello, do you speak frock?').

No wonder we're bewildered. What we call a size 12 is called 40 in France, 42 in Italy, 38 in Germany – and 'extra small' in the United States. Don't you love the idea of 12 being 'extra small'? I always thought it was more like 'biggest you can admit to'. Mind you, this chart is supposed to be underwear sizes, which are probably calculated by adding your glove size to your hat size and taking away your shoe size.

Certainly I was always led to believe that American sizes were just one smaller than ours, so that what is really a 12 is labelled a 10. So how come my American clothes are 6s and 8s?

Because Donna and Ralph and Calvin are really smart. This simple detail is why they are all so rich. There is nothing that wing-ding about their clothes really, but anything with a size 6 label which (a) does up and (b) looks half decent is going to be coming home with me. It's genius. (And Donna Karan seems to know all about being a fat girl in the changing room, since her clothes seem to be the most creatively sized of them all.)

I don't know why more Australian designers don't get wise to this scam. In fact, many of them, especially the groovy woovy ones on the Chapel Street/Oxford Street strips, seem to go the other way. It's as if they want us to feel bad in their clothes.

I love Alannah Hill's fey-floozy clothes, for example, but they are so tiny I can't even shoehorn myself into a 14. This does not make me feel like going back to her shop. Ever. And I couldn't help noticing in a recent sale that all the Alannah Hill stuff that was left over was size 8. Ner ner, ner ner ner. Doesn't she get it? Surely I am not the only woman with breasts in Australia who would like to wear a lace-edged 1940s-style afternoon dress.

If I were a fashion designer I wouldn't have sizes in my clothes at all. I'd call them 'You Babe' (16), 'Foxy Lady' (14), 'Dream Machine' (12), 'Ooh La La!' (10) and 'You Bitch' (8). So my customers wouldn't feel at all shy about saying, 'This is a bit tight on the wrists. Do you have it in a Foxy Lady? Great, I'll take two.'

And then I could have a beach house in the Hamptons right next to Donna's.

Not so smart casual

I have made a measured and considered decision to stop wearing my pyjamas to the office. They're not really pyjamas, of course, but they might as well be. The problem is that wearing stretch pants, jersey tops and slip-on shoes, however chic and designer and expensive, I feel as though I'm in pyjamas, which leads to a tendency to behave as though I'm in pyjamas. Zzzzzzzz . . .

So that's all over. No more elastic waists to work, it's hopeless for productivity. I'm going back to wearing jackets to the office. Jackets, with tailored skirts or pants. Oh! I remember those things – we used to wear them in the twentieth century and we called them 'suits'. Quaint though it seems, there was something about wearing a suit to work that used to make me sit up straighter. Because I felt smart – I felt, you know, smart. I think my IQ drops about ten points when I come to work in a T-shirt.

I blame America for this. It was American corporations that started the wretched notion of Casual Friday. Or was it American law firms? Who cares, either way it was a very sorry day when some fat-bellied Yank came up with the idea of wearing golf clothes to work on Friday to make the segue to Connecticut weekend wear that little bit smoother.

That's one theory for how it started. The other is that, like everything else since 1995, it began in Silicon Valley, where both arms of the IT brotherhood – the hip cat swinger skateboarding techno dudes and the never-been-kissed drip-dry nerds – insisted on wearing their tribal colours to work. That's shorts and gnarly sandshoes for one lot and easy-care DriCel pull-on separates for the other.

Terrified of being left behind, the dinosaurish old corporations relaxed their workplace dress codes to match, hoping to entice thrusting young dot coms to come to work for them. And as the rest of the world copies America as unthinkingly as a toddler helping Daddy fill the supermarket trolley, now we're all wearing weekend wear to work, too.

And because human beings are fundamentally lazy carcasses, Casual Friday has turned into Slobby Every Day. The offices where I work are beginning to look more like a day at the seaside than a day at the corporate coalface. My colleagues in the fourth estate are wearing Birkenstock sandals, combat pants, Hawaiian shirts, skimpy summer dresses and even rubber thongs to work. I fear winter – who will be first to turn up in fleecy trackie daks and ug boots? You couldn't get into a Kings Cross nightclub in half these outfits, but suddenly it's okay to wear them to work at a leading newspaper.

Well, it's not okay. Apart from the fact that it's like being surrounded by superannuated adolescents in I'm-not-combing-my-hair-for-granny outfits, Slobby Every Day cuts out the crucial signalling function of work clothes. How was I to know that the fellow in shorts and combat boots was . . . well, quite important on the paper? To me he looked like a resting actor bringing around one of those sandwich baskets, and I really didn't appreciate his butting in on our meeting.

And there is another reason why I am revolting against the relaxation of corporate dress codes: treading the sartorial highwire between relaxed executive and functioning derelict makes getting dressed in the morning a total nightmare. Everyone knows 'smart casual' is the hardest look to do. Why on earth would you want to inflict it upon yourself every day of your working life?

So for all these reasons, I'm going back to the Maoist pragmatism of suits. Three suits, five shirts, two pairs of shoes and that will be my working wardrobe worked out. All I've got to do now is find three suits comfortable enough to sit down in all day.

Hobgoblin heels

Quite by chance I have stumbled on the key to an international mystery. It came upon me in a shoe shop in rue du Cherche-Midi in Paris, centre of the shoe universe. I was looking at the pale pink patent pumps with toes like platypus bills, and red shorty ankle boots with ultra-flat splayed circular heels, and heard myself say: 'These are the shoes hobgoblins wear to parties. And this is the dance they do in them . . .'

As I assumed the correct stance to demonstrate the Hobgoblin Stomp, I saw that my friend Victoria had simultaneously put herself into exactly the same position. She Just Knew. Suddenly the whole thing became clear – hobgoblins have taken over world shoe manufacture and that's why shops are currently full of things only they would want to wear.

Anyway, here's how you do the dance: bend your knees into an inelegant crouch, then raise your legs alternately, with feet turned harshly up – the better to show off your lime green ponyskin clogs. Arms are held out to the side, mean fists raised, and you slide your eyes slowly from side to side as you do it. Hobgoblins have such flat faces that this is the only way they can see who is coming up on the outside – which is important, as they get blind on mead at their hoedowns and any dance-floor collisions lead to ugly fights.

Coalmining and blacksmithing were the traditional hobgoblin trades until a consultant from McKinsey's told them they needed to diversify – and that's when they started producing these terrible shoes. Mind you, when you consider what else hobgoblins wear, the shoes start to make sense. All hobgoblins – male and female – wear skirts and, although their body shape makes Danny DeVito look willowy, they favour the dirndl, the more sticky-out the better. The fashionable young hobettes were very excited about the ski wear in a recent Chanel show – thickly padded bell-shaped skirts.

Hobgoblins' hair is multicoloured and worn tied up in plaits above their ears, which have very pendulous lobes. Slobodan Milosevic is a hobgoblin who came up from the caverns below Belgrade, cut off his plaits and had surgery on his ear lobes – and so is Madeleine Albright. Although they don't get on in their human guises, you may see them by the light of the waning moon, dancing the Hobgoblin Stomp, with red and turquoise platform cowboy boots on their stumpy hobgoblin feet.

But as well as these ghastly hobs, there is one benign force also at work in the world producing shoes – the Shoe Fairy. She is responsible for all the pink and mauve mules currently on sale. If you see a shoe with an impossibly waisted heel and an ickle pretty bow on the toe, she made it. She's a ditz. Her shoes are all divine, but – along with her close relative Manolo Blahnik – she doesn't have much of a grip on reality. She has wings, so her calfskin soles never actually touch the ground; she just floats along 2 millimetres above it and if she ever needs to get anywhere in a hurry, she just grabs hold of a passing butterfly. Thus she has no idea of the pain and suffering her adorable shoes cause their human wearers.

So that explains the two extremes of shoes currently on sale, but there is one part of the mystery yet to be solved: what have the horrible hobgobs done with the kindly old shoemaker who used to oversee the elves who made all the practical, yet attractive, shoes we used to be able to buy? I suspect they are holding him captive in an underground cell, while the elves (a sweet but undisciplined lot) sit idle without his guidance.

Any information leading to his return gratefully received.

All strung out

There is something worse than the Visible Panty Line – the Visible G-String Line. I suppose we should call it a VGSL. (Funny coincidence how it reads like an acronym for some kind of genital ointment, isn't it? Especially as you feel as if you need something soothing down there after wearing one.)

Anyway, a VGSL is like having a billboard plastered across your arse saying, 'I didn't want to have a visible panty line under this form-fitting cotton Lycra dress so I'm wearing a G-string. I'M WEARING A G-STRING. GOT IT?' This look is particularly grotesque under tight white trousers. The sight of such a posterior wiggling along the street brings to mind all too clearly images of what my friend V. calls 'chewing cloth'. And surely I don't need to remind you what they call G-strings in Brazil . . . Oh, all right then. Dental floss.

G-strings are awful. Women who say they are 'more comfortable' than proper knickers are the same brand of gender traitors who used to say they wore stockings and suspenders because they were 'more comfortable'.

Oh, please, how could having your legs attached to your hips by snapping elastic possibly be comfortable? You feel like a puppet. Dance, Pinocchio, dance. Suspender belts are vile contraptions. They're not underclothing, they're apparatus. They are equipment. I only know how uncomfortable they are because, in my youth, I had a boyfriend who thought stockings and suspenders were heaven (he had a 1940s fixation generally, but he also played the saxophone and dressed like Robert de Niro in *New York, New York*, so you can see why I thought it was worth it). I'm happy to say I haven't met a man my age since who went ga-ga for garter belts. Apart from pervy types who enjoy the readers' wives section of *Penthouse* magazine, it seems to be a fetish that has run its course. Good riddance.

In fact, most guys I know actively dislike stockings. 'Sluttish' was a word that came up when I canvassed opinion among some red-blooded chaps of my acquaintance. Some of them even said they find tights (which I have always thought were a fairly effective contraceptive) sexy, probably because that is what they found the first time they put their hand up a girl's skirt at the pictures. And do you know what else these fellows said they find a big

18

turn-off? That's right, G-strings. They appear to make men almost as uncomfortable as they make us. There's some kind of *Cleo*-reading multiple-orgasm expectation implicit in them that makes blokes want to go home and watch go-kart racing. (Although one of my sources did add that G-strings can be acceptable on 'a perfect Coppertone bottom', which was big-hearted of him.)

I know there are men out there who get the Victoria's Secret catalogues air-freighted over from the States and someone must be keeping La Perla in business, but the undergarment genre the sophisticated men-about-town I talked to professed to like best are simple white Cottontail knickers. Elvis lives. And, one of them added, unprompted, 'The line of them over the hip under a pair of tight trousers is gorgeous.' Hang on – isn't he describing a VPL? So there you have it. All those chicks pretending they like walking around with a cheese wire up their clacker because they thought G-strings were supposed to be sexy and it turns out men liked VPLs all the time.

Of course the choice of underscunder is not entirely about dressing (or undressing) for men. There is the fine line of your Easton Pearson evening dress to think about, too. But if you are still worried about your knickers showing under your clothes, there is one simple and comfortable solution. Don't wear any. (Ask any Scotsman.)

Crowning glory

Could we be hats? It's just a thought, but the whole accessories thing is just getting bigger and bigger and it seems like the obvious progression. I am now as fully obsessed with handbags as I have always been with shoes. A lingering fetish for scarves is fast turning into a full-blown mania, and suddenly it seems – hats, I want them.

Not just sunhats to keep off the UV rays (incidentally, have you seen a recent photo of the sun-loving Princess Stephanie? You could make a leather Akubra out of her forehead) or once-a-year hats for the races, but dress hats for lunch, cocktail hats for cocktails and charming little hatty confections to wear out to dinner. In other words, glamour hats for every day – like women used to wear, up until some point in the 1960s when we threw the notion to the four winds, along with our toques, berets, cloches, pillboxes, bowlers, boaters and bonnets. I want mine back.

My great friend B., who was editor of the British equivalent of *The Australian Women's Weekly* in the late 1950s, tells me they all wore hats – and gloves – to work every day back then. It would have been unthinkable not to, she says. That could be a teensy-weensy little bit of a bore (ever tried typing in gloves?), but when I asked a group of friends at a smart dinner recently if they wished we were all sitting there in darling little hats, they squealed with delight at the prospect. So what's stopping us?

Even high fashion has given the notion a bit of a nod. In one of my favourite ever collections for Miu Miu, which was so atmospheric it was more like a short story than a fashion show, Miuccia Prada finished the look for her mournful young woman, circa 1950, with a wonderfully characterful hat (and a suitcase).

One look at that hat and I had the whole story: forced to work as a maid after losing her family in the war, Marie-Louise was heading for the station to seek her fortune in Paris. That beaten-up old thing was the only hat she had – a last crumpled piece of dignity on her beautiful young head. (In my fevered imagination, she went on to become the toast of *le tout* Paris for the magnificent chapeaux she created for her hat salon, Maison Marie-Louise, after

21

finding a black ostrich feather on a street in Le Marais . . .
It gets boring at fashion shows.)

But high fashion aside, I know I'm not alone in this hat-fancying thing. Not long after that show I went to the charity auction of the spectacular wardrobe of retired Sydney socialite Betty Rose McInerney (vintage Givenchy for miles), expecting to romp home with swags of her exquisite Paris hats, only to find myself in a room full of women already wearing gorgeous headgear – on a Sunday afternoon – and clearly intent on adding to their collections.

Bidding was furious on all ninety-two hats, and the two I particularly craved – a black velvet pillbox with a veil and an ostrich feather, and a very Audrey H. velvet coolie-style number – went for $240 and $950 respectively (not to me).

As there are clearly plenty of other women out there who adore the idea of having a feather in their caps, all we need to do is have the guts to start wearing them again. Simple. There are so many reasons why it's a good idea. Unlike other cult accessories, you can just have fun with hats without worrying about any dreary practical considerations, like walking, or having room for your Palm Pilot. If you're wearing a hat, it doesn't matter if your hair is as dirty as a biker's denims. They involve such gorgeous notions as gossamer wisps of veil, saucy bunches of cherries and even tiny little birds. Hat pins.

That's settled then – the glamour cocktail hat is back. So you go first and I'll follow, okay?

Fashion eats itself

'Stop the fashion system!' absurdist fashion designer Franco Moschino used to implore. What a shame he didn't live to see it happen, because fashion seems to have stopped itself. Nothing is out of fashion any more. Even hemlines, for so long the most fundamental of all fashion barometers, are no longer an issue.

Look at any group of women and you are likely to see skirts stopping everywhere from the bottom of their shoes to the bottom of their bottoms. There isn't even a hemline convention for trousers any more. It's just, you know, whatever.

This unfashion phenomenon really struck me when I was writing one of these columns the other week. I was trying to come up with an example of something really dated and sad to get a cheap laugh, and my mind was blank. There was nothing funny enough to poke fun at. In the 1980s you just had to whisper the word 'flares' to have everyone rolling around in embarrassed hilarity. 'Oh no!' we used to cry. 'Seventies clothes! Agh! Body shirts! Slacks! White shoes! What we all looked like!'

All those things look fine to me now. So does 1960s hippie gear – I'd love one of those Kashmiri mirrored dresses and an Afghan coat. And I adore my 50s fake leopard-skin coat and my flowery 40s dress. In the end, the best I could do was make fun of 80s shoulder pads (well, I did have them in my bras and nighties, which was a bit much). But I couldn't think of anything from the 90s to make fun of. Now, that is weird.

Think of the big trends of the past decade and rate their cringe value. Bootleg pants? I still wear them. Cardigans over petticoat dresses? Still looks cute to me. Pashmina shawls? I intend to die wrapped in one. Pedal pushers? Fine for hot/cold days. Cargo pants? Wearing 'em right now, buddy. Grunge? People wear cargo pants to the office . . . Prada? Gimme gimme.

I might not be in a great rush to buy any more of those across-the-body ergonomic handbags with special pockets for your mobile phone and your bike padlock, but the thought of them doesn't reduce me instantly to the quivering dead-fly position. I don't nudge my friends and point at people in the street who are wearing them. And when I go to New York in winter, I'm still going to wear my thick-soled pod shoes to survive in the freezing weather. None of it's madly 'in' or madly 'out'. It's all just stuff.

You know how this happened? Fashion ate itself. The 90s was the revivals decade and the reviving has just got faster and faster, until we have reached the point where things are revived so quickly they don't have a chance to fully go out before they come in again.

It took the whole of the 1970s for flares to go out completely, which is why we found them so universally risible by 1980. When they came back in about 1994, they were already going out with the early uptake fashion victims before the majority of the population had even got their heads around the idea of wearing them again.

As a result, they've been left suspended in fashion limbo, not particularly in, but not spectacularly out either.

The same thing is happening now with black trouser suits. While they were already totally O-V-E-R in high-fashion circles (where women were dressing like Latvian shepherdesses on strong pharmaceuticals), the sharp black suit, white T-shirt and open shoes thing was just gaining real currency with the masses. Then it started to come back in again from the big designers . . .

And so we have ended up in Moschino's fashion-free nirvana – where you can wear whatever you damn well please. Although I can think of one thing that's really, really OUT: In and Out lists.

The small print

Wouldn't it be great if clothes came with instructions? I don't just mean washing instructions – they're mostly a waste of space, erring so strongly on the unsueable side of caution that I have seen underpants bearing labels saying 'Dry clean only'. And they never say anything useful, like 'Fabric will develop unattractive bobbles on first wearing', or 'Liable to cause body odour in the excitable'.

Despite these failings, washing instructions do have their uses. Just this morning I had reached the till with a very cosy polar fleece bathrobe when I noticed the words 'Hand wash only in cold water' on the care label. As if. The thing was the size of Barry White's fat-day kaftan. I'd have to hand wash it in Sydney Harbour and get it airlifted into the spinner. So those washing instructions saved me from a long whiffy winter in an unwashed bathrobe.

But what I'd really like to see are *wearing* instructions. They could start by telling you which part of your body the garment is meant to cover and have arrows to show which way is up. The more 'creative' the designer, the harder this generally is to figure out. A built-in compass could be useful. Or those illuminated emergency arrows they have on the floor of aeroplanes.

In a sad attempt to wear more 'interesting' clothes, I once tried on something by Comme des Garçons. It looked like a little cardigan and a long skirt on the hanger, but when I got it into the changing room it had shape shifted, like a sorceress, into something tailor made for a very slim dromedary.

Once I had it on, the cardigan appeared to be wider than it was high and I wasn't even sure I had my head through the right hole. Fastening the skirt required the assistance of a civil engineer, or a master of origami. Even getting it back on the hanger was an aptitude test. Running out of the shop was easy, though.

That was my last attempt with 'art' clothing. Now I stick to garments I could make myself with paper and crayons for a cut-out doll. (Does anyone else remember cut-out dolls, incidentally?)

If I don't know the name for it – skirt, shirt, trousers, vest, poncho, tabard etc. – I don't even consider it. My other guideline is: 'Have to tie it? Don't buy it.' Those are my shopping rules and they have made life much easier than trying on clothes more physically demanding than a game of Twister.

But even my cut-out dolly clothes could be improved with some simple instructions stitched into the lining. The red trackpants I am wearing as I write could say, for example: 'Not to be worn out of the house.' My lovely bias-cut scarf-silk skirt could have a little label in the seam saying: 'Won't go with any other garment ever made.' And my black jersey DKNY pants would be doing everyone a favour if they had a label warning: 'Not to be worn more than seven times a week.'

I could even do with some more instructive help from my beautiful dark red ostrich-leather-style coat (couldn't possibly afford the real thing and suspect it may be illegal anyway). It is my most favourite thing in the world at the moment, but so far I've only managed to wear it once, because how many occasions can you think of where you can keep your coat on indoors without making people nervous?

A label explaining 'Only suitable for Paris fashion shows or a day at the races with limousine transfer' might have made me think twice about sinking my life savings into a useless piece of spotty leather. Or it could be something even simpler (and the same label would have worked with that polar fleece bathrobe, which would cut costs for manufacturers): 'You'll regret it' would work for about 50 per cent of my wardrobe.

The beauty myth

Stressed out, worn out, feeling plain? A little bit spotty, a little bit lumpy and hairy in all the wrong places? Is your nose veinous? Is your chin grey? Go on, treat yourself! You deserve it! Indulge in our top-to-toe package of luxurious beauty treatments and you will emerge feeling . . . suicidal, actually.

Pampering is a myth. It doesn't work. Well, it does work, as long as you are feeling great to begin with. A deep-cleansing facial would be the umbrella in the pina colada if you and your lithe, hairless body have just spent a week lying on the beach reading books by Dominick Dunne ('As a matter of fact,' said Laetitia, her hand gripping the Christofle letter opener, 'he's not my butler. He's my father') and Jilly Cooper ('Gosh,' gasped Hattie, her soft cheeks turning a darker shade of beetroot. 'I think you touched my fetlock').

But if you've had a normal week – drivers who pull out in front of you without indicating and then immediately turn off, a ringing mobile lost in the bottom of your handbag, your favourite pedal pushers back from the dry cleaners with creases in them – a spot of pampering could be just the thing to tip you over from normal urban angst into full-scale millennium psychosis.

It starts the moment you walk, scowling, into the subtly lit Oasis du Beauté. The first thing someone does is be nice to you. Don't they know how annoying that is? And why is everybody whispering?

From there it just gets worse. As the coltish nymphette with perfect nails and glowing skin lisps a patronising greeting, she slips another Enya CD into the sound system and pours a fresh litre of essential oils into the infuser. Reeling from the aromatherapeutic effects of rose, geranium and tangelo (nausea, stinging eyes and instant asthma), you are asked to take off all your clothes, put them on a wire hanger and lie motionless for two hours in a very cold room while various unpleasant things are done to you.

Pampering involves having your blackheads squeezed, stinging dye applied to your eyelashes, ingrowing hairs lanced with scalpels, scalding steam directed up your nose, dry skin lathed from the soles of your feet with terrifying blades, cuticles cut despite all protests, delicate eye areas roughly handled and your eyebrows pulled out by the roots. What is relaxing about any of that?

Often the worst part is the complimentary neck and shoulder massage you have been fantasising about all day. A disappointing neck rub is even more frustrating than blah sex, because you can't finish it off for yourself. And if you are feeling a little bit sad and the massage is quite good, the tender touch of a stranger can make you burst into tears. Not pampering, but whimpering.

After all this, you emerge not the airbrushed vision you'd imagined, but a red-eyed turnip having a bad hair day. That's $150, please.

So this is my advice to the overworked, overweight and overwrought: leave the pampering for when your self-esteem is up to it. The rest of the time, just eat chocolate.

A good sort

My mother calls it 'filing'. Whenever she's feeling a bit out of sorts and humphy she goes off and tidies a drawer, rearranges her jumper cupboard or, as in a recent humungous effort, entirely sorts out The Untidy Room. This is a small room in her house (briefly called 'the study') where we all put things we don't know what to do with. Sometimes I just open the door, throw in the offending item and close it very quickly. (Please don't tell her.)

There is also a shed in the garden next to the greenhouse which is full of my books and boxes of mystery objects. Every time I go home I perform the Ancient Ceremony of the Shed, which involves the Finding of the Key, followed by the solemn Opening of the Door, the Realisation of the Horror (too many rakes, staves and broken garden chairs between me and *Winnie the Pooh*) and then the Closing of the Door.

There are other boxes in the garage and some of my furniture, but this is all so shrouded with cobwebs, we just pretend it isn't there. Miss Haversham would think it needed a bit of a spring clean. But it works for us. My mother has hung a strawberry punnet from the roof on a piece of string so you know where to stop the car just before driving into my chest of drawers.

Then there is the attic, which is full of suitcases and boxes of Christmas decorations. There is something very poignant about dusty hat boxes and ancient plastic bags full of tinsel. About once every two years I brave it up there, opening my trunk of vintage clothes, sighing over it all and closing it again. I usually find one thing I can throw away.

Last time it was a pinstripe suit jacket I bought at a jumble sale that had been made by a Savile Row tailor. For the Michelin Man. It was enormous, but so beautiful. I used to wear it in the early 80s with an arrangement of kilt pins and thought it looked terribly Japanese. Probably looked bonkers, but it was still hard to throw it out.

Sometimes I also remove some treasure like a pair of flared Wrangler jeans with embroidered back pockets (size: mini me), or brown platform brogues from Sacha circa 1975, and give them to whichever niece happens to be downstairs.

Now I am establishing my own system in my latest home. This place is a warren of interesting storage possibilities. There is a big dusty cupboard under the stairs that makes me feel completely at home. Then there are two big cupboards in the roof cavity in the bedroom which were just meant for suitcases, hat boxes and storing winter clothes. I have had such a jolly time filing winter shoes into wire baskets and zipping cashmere jumpers into moth-proof bags. Adding to my joy, I've had special shelves built along the bottom of one wardrobe, just the right size for shoe boxes.

All this activity was made even more satisfying by the discovery of a shop that sells nothing but gadgets to aid efficient storage – all American, of course. I am now the proud owner of a bra sorter, which is a plastic box that enables you to arrange them in neat horizontal lines, so you can select the one you want without disturbing the others, rather than go rifling through the drawer like a cat in a litter tray.

Small things, I know, but having a bra sorter somehow makes the mad mungo chaos of the rest of life easier to deal with. The news is full of catastrophe, but at least I can find my best burgundy bra when I need it.

And now I'm off to tidy a drawer.

Hee Bee Gee Bees

I don't need drink and drugs to get me in the party mood. Oh no. Just put me in front of a Bee Gees video and I'll be happy for hours. It was Barry Gibb's trousers that did it. White flares. Python tight around the upper thigh with perfect testicular definition. Lift and separate. Do you think he ever appeared in public in them, or were they only allowed out for video clips?

Those pervy pants would have been bad enough in any colour, but the amazing petrochemical whiteness of them made it all so much more startling. The only thing whiter than those pants were his alarming teeth, which would appear suddenly, snapping on like an outdoor security light, whenever he trilled a particularly testing vibrato aaaaaaaah, as in 'Stayin' alive . . . aaaaaaaah!' The connection between those tourniquet trews and his castrato singing style is so apparent it hardly needs to be pointed out. Aaaaaaaah!

I may have found them risible, but Barry clearly thought he looked terrific in those trousers because he wore a similar pair in the clip for 'How Deep Is Your Love?'. Well, that's not a question you'd need to ask Barry, is it? One look at them pants and you know exactly how deep his love is.

Another feature of both the Bee Gees videos I was lucky enough to see the other night was a back view of the three brothers walking away, so that everyone could see Barry's bum in the white pants and the other two Gibbs could see how much shorter than him they were. And how much flatter their hair was. Oh the hair! In 1978 each Gibb brother had one of the three tonsorial looks I most fear on bad hair days: bouffy, pancake and bald.

Barry's hilarious hair is shown to particular effect in the clip for 'How Big Is Your Do?'. The opening shot is a full-screen close-up of his goaty head, and bouffant hardly describes it. It's had more coats of lacquer than a vintage Rolls Royce. He could have used it as a crash helmet. A percussion instrument. A nut cracker. The extraordinary thing is he looks very pleased with the whole arrange-ment, but I suppose when you take in the unfortunate brothers it puts it all into perspective. In the land of the ug, the boufhead man is king.

Anyway, straight after the Bee Gees – it was a 1978 video theme night – came a clip for a disco funk band (name forgotten) singing 'Dance – Dance Dance Dance', which includes the memorable passage 'yowser yowser yowser, I wanna boogie wid you . . .' Their outfits weren't crash hot either. The men wore those 1970s/1930s revival gangster suits with thigh huggin' pants nastily tailored in 100 per cent man-mades, worn too long. Yowser yowser yowser, where d'ya get dem trouser? I was moved to wonder. The gals wore spandex cat suits of unforgiving cut.

All of which made me reflect that either 1978 was a particularly tragic year for pop videos, or 70s clothes are actually far worse than we remember them now. This is all very confusing because I spent most of the 80s laughing at the clothes people used to wear in the 70s and then most of the 90s wearing revivals of them. I couldn't wait to get back into flares, platforms and body shirts in 1994. Mad for them.

But after watching those videos last night I have realised that our idea of what people actually wore in the 70s has become rosy with time. The constant revivals of 70s looks actually have as much to do with real 70s clothes as those frightful double-breasted Yowser Yowser suits had to do with the 1930s, or the costumes for *Grease* had to do with what people actually looked like in the 1950s. Not a lot.

And funnily enough *Grease* was also made in 1978. So maybe it was just a dud year.

And that was Hat . . .

I lost my hat. Not metaphorically, at the racetrack, but really. A gust of wind blew my beloved straw stetson off my head when I was standing on a high bluff looking over Kings Canyon in the Northern Territory.

It was a fine way for it to go. I wasn't standing, actually. I was lying on the ground composing a pretentious art photo and my old hat thought, Sod this for a game of soldiers, can't be doing with this arty-farty claptrap, I'm off. And away it went, up and out, high on a breeze, to land who knows where. Running after it was never an option, being about 99 centimetres from the edge of a major cliff at the time. It really picked its moment.

And it didn't half give my fellow hikers a surprise as it flew past them where they were standing in an obedient group, not taking art photos, around the corner. In no time, the guide had whipped out his binocs and found Hat's resting place under a tree halfway down the canyon. It looked quite at home there.

I think they all expected me to weep and wail and demand a helicopter rescue, but I just blew old Hat a kiss and carried on walking. It's what Hat would have wanted.

Of course, I was sad to say goodbye. That hat was the first thing I bought when I moved to Australia in 1993. I bought it from Vic Cooper Hats, 'Sydney's Oldest Hat Shop', in the Royal Arcade, in full intention of it being a Hat For Life.

From then on it was a feature of every weekend away, every trip to the beach and most outdoor activities. It enjoyed picnics, polo and poolside parties over five Sydney summers and went round the world with me several times, too. We were laughed at on a Bali beach, went to a party in the Daintree rainforest and spent a glorious week lounging around on a white coral island in the Philippines. I don't think many other stetsons have been scuba diving.

But while Hat didn't mind the high life, our favourite trips together were up to the tiny village of Nundle in the NSW north country where we yee-hawed at the rodeo, nudging each other and sneaking sideways looks at all the gorgeous cowboys and their hats. I don't have many holiday snaps from the 1990s that don't feature Hat.

A hat like that, with all the dents and dints of shared

experience, is much more than an accessory, it's more like a friend. But you also have to accept that it's not just an object that you can possess. It has a life of its own and it was time for it to move on.

I hope a family of echidnas sets up house under that sheltering crown. I hope whole tribes of ants march over the top of it on their busy anty business. I hope a brown snake curls itself around the brim and has a snooze in the sun. I just hope a passing wallaroo doesn't land on it hard and squash it to bits. And if it blows down to a more accessible place and some passing walker picks it up and wears it, I hope they will have as much fun together as we did.

The funny thing is I think I must have known it was going to go because, just minutes before lift-off, I noticed what a fine silhouette Hat's shadow made against the rock and stopped to take a photo of our shadows together.

When I got the prints back, it looked as if I was waving goodbye.

If I were a chic man

Sometimes I really wish I were a man. I wish this particularly when I can't get dressed in the morning because my bosoms are getting in the way and there are just too many choices and I think of all the blokes at work who just wear suits and ties every day. It's so easy for them. No-one ever missed the bus agonising over which tie to wear.

And I love men's clothes. All the thrilling different shirtings you can get in five-million-ways-with-a-stripe and those tiny little differences in the shape of collars that make such a big difference to your image.

I would wear cutaway collars if I were a bloke. And handmade striped shirts which Juanita, my maid, would iron for me. And only ever Hermès ties. And those wonderful tailor-made Richard James suits, which are secretly lined with fuchsia silk and have two back vents which swish up when you walk quickly. I would always walk quickly.

I'd have gold cufflinks with my monogram on them and a signet ring on the little finger of my left hand and those really heavy Church's brogues. In black. (I'd also be 190 centimetres tall and a millionaire, so let me dream.)

At the weekend I would wear flat-front chinos, with round-neck T-shirts and cashmere V-neck jumpers with no welt at the bottom, so they would just hang down straight with little side slits. I'd wear Gucci loafers with no socks to show off my hairy brown ankles. I'd have a fierce pair of brown suede cowboy boots tucked away somewhere, too.

Sometimes I would just wear really old Levi's with an old polo shirt, collar up. And I'd have a really, really good watch. I'd have a gorgeous leather jacket in a reefer style and a big heavy silver key ring with the keys to my old Jag on it.

On really cold days I'd wear a knitted watch cap, like Jack Nicholson in *The Last Detail*, and a yellow cashmere scarf. I'd drink single malts. And I might have a dog like the one in *The Thin Man*. I'd definitely have a dressing-gown like the man in *The Thin Man*.

I would sleep in the nude and wear white Y-fronts and sometimes striped cotton boxer shorts. I'd play soccer and poker and be really, really good at pinball.

I'd shave, using a badger brush and a blade, with a very

white towel wrapped around my waist. I'd have a tattoo. Somewhere. And my old girlfriends would swoon any time they caught a whiff of Guerlain's Vetiver because it would remind them of me.

I'd have an old dinner jacket I bought in a second-hand shop in London and a very old, very floppy black silk bow tie, which would always be undone and hanging down by the end of the evening because I would be hot from all the dancing. I'd have jet studs in my starched-front dinner shirt and evening shoes polished to a high shine. I'd shrug my overcoat over my shoulders. I'd look pretty good in a kilt, too.

I'd have an old Guernsey sweater for sailing, whites for tennis and Speedo swimming trunks saying Bondi on the bum. I'd wear a flower in my buttonhole at the races and a sarong to dinner on holiday.

If I were a man, I'd have longish sideboards and a side parting, a bit floppy on the top. I'd look really good with wet hair and one day's growth after the gym on Sundays. I wouldn't have my shoulders waxed but I would keep an eye on uninvited nose hair.

If I were a man, I would polish my shoes and always have a clean cotton hanky in my pocket.

If I were a man, I'd never leave the lavatory seat up and, if I were a man, I'd marry me.

The wrong trousers

Talk about the wrong trousers. I had the wrong trousers, the wrong shoes and, in particular, the wrong dry cleaners.

Oh, I felt so cool, spinning up to the ABC's Gore Hill studio to tape my second appearance on 'O'Loghlin on Saturday Night'. Television, smellyvision, done it a million times (well, maybe twenty-five), I know what to wear. Not stripes or geometric patterns because they 'jazz', not black because it just goes into a blob, not white unless you want to look like you're singing in a gospel choir.

I was so laid back about it all I just dropped by my dry cleaners on the way to the studio ('studio') to pick up a couple of pairs of pants to sling into the back of the car along with my choice of Armani and Equipment shirts (one navy blue chiffon, one snakeskin print, both dead groovy), and a wild selection of shoe-en.

I had selected a pant-and-shirt combo particularly because the last time I went on the show I wore my best dress. It's a gorgeous frock but I soon discovered why not many people wear dresses on television. There's no waist-band to hang the microphone powerpack off, and they were forced to rig me out with this thing like a 1950s sanitary belt to hold it in place.

So I had to make my big entrance down the steps in front of a live audience, terrified it was going to slide down my hips and make a special guest appearance between my legs. Very relaxing. Hello, Mum.

So this time it was all going to be perfect. I hung my gear up in my dressing room in its dry-cleaning bags and went to chill with the guys in the Green Room, before cruising into Make-up with the nice ladies who knew me from last time. I was so at home I made Richard Wilkins look like Mr Bean. Catch you on the flip side, baby.

Then I went to get changed. La la la. Should I wear the black jersey pants or the grey jersey pants? Oh. The black jersey pants weren't the swingy bell bottoms I thought they were. They were my cropped pants. Not a good look with the range of strappy stilettos I'd brought with me as feature shoes. Okay then, the grey, with the snake, with the Michel Perry hologram silver spikes. Beauty.

Not. When I wrestled them from the plastic covering, my very expensive grey jersey Halston-style flares turned out to be size 4 half-mast gaucho pantalones. They'd shrunk 30 centimetres in the leg and about 10 around the waist. It was ten minutes to showtime and there was only one thing I could do. I panicked.

Fortunately, the producer happened by when I was doing an impression of Munch's *The Scream* in the corridor and he sent Natalie from Wardrobe to look after me. Cool, calm and collected, Natalie took one look at the shoes, one look at the wrong trousers, agreed I was a total disaster and marched me straight down the concrete corridors to the ABC wardrobe. This is not as good as it sounds. For a moment I thought I was going to be appearing as B1. His costume was the best thing they had on offer down there.

But among the massed ranks of police uniforms, polyester dresses, padded blue-and-white striped pyjamas, banana heads and dear little Ratty noses (like a fun fur fez on elastic), Natalie found one rogue pair of black Emporio Armani trousers. The right trousers. A size or two too small and several metres too long, but no problem, we had at least three minutes to shorten them and to find a safety pin large enough to fasten the waist.

And so I made my entrance in somebody else's pants, slightly shaken, but equally stirred – by the row I was planning to have with my dry cleaners in the morning.

The meaning of like

The press and buyers at the European fashion shows have a language entirely their own. 'Genius' has nothing to do with discovering the cure for cancer: it's a fair description of the latest Gucci heel shape. 'Working back' doesn't mean staying late in the office: it describes ways of accessorising an outfit to make the clothes look less boring and ordinary, as in 'I'll be working back the camel suit with the Prada brogue mule in the bilberry.'

But this fashion lingo – flingo – is never more abstract than when you ask someone's opinion as you are all leaving a show. Saying the wrong thing could lose you crucial advertising/an exclusive retail account/your reputation in an instant. So a special obtuse code has been developed. As you walk out of the abandoned factory/disused fire station/scrap heap where a show has been held, you will hear the following responses to the question: 'What did you think of that?' And here is what they really mean . . .

- 'There were some nice pieces.' (Really means: It was incredibly boring, but they advertise in the magazine, so I'll have to find a white shirt or some godforsaken thing I can use to give them an editorial credit. Or sometimes it means: It looked hideous to me, but I'm not confident to say so. What if everybody else loved it? Or: I loved it, but I want to see what Suzy Menkes says about it before I admit to it. What if everyone else hated it?)
- 'It was quite pretty.' (It was boring.)
- 'It was pretty.' (It was boring, but they advertise.)
- 'It was really pretty.' (It was pretty. Really boring, but pretty. If you like pastels.)
- 'It was really, really pretty.' (It had a lot of gypsy embroidery and harem skirts and I feel like doing a fashion trip to Morocco.)
- 'It was a bit predictable.' (I fell asleep. And when I woke up, a bride was coming down the runway.)
- 'It was really commercial.' (It was indescribably boring.)
- 'It was quite classic.' (It was indescribably boring, but they are advertisers. We'll definitely be doing a white shirts story.)
- 'It was fabulous.' (It was fabulous.)

- 'It was genius.' (It was fabulous and I get a discount.)
- 'I loved it. I love Dries.' (I didn't like it that much, but he sent me a fabulous free handbag this week.)
- 'I know I can make it work in-store.' (I think the designer has been taking some mind-altering drugs. I'll force him to make me a black suit the same as last season's or they'll lose the account.)
- 'It wasn't bad.' (It was awful.)
- 'It was great.' (It's going to fit my big bum.)
- 'I thought it was adorable.' (I thought it was tragic, but the designer is a really good friend of mine. Well, we had lunch once.)
- 'It was tragic.' (They just pulled their advertising – and after I featured that hideous black skirt last month, the ingrates.)
- 'I missed it because I had an appointment at Dolce.' (It's always gruesome and I went shopping instead. But they advertise. I really hope they did some white shirts.)
- 'It was pretty blah.' (They gave me a seat in the seventh row.)
- 'It was a waste of time.' (They gave me a standing-only ticket.)
- 'I couldn't go. I had to go to an appointment at Fendi and they don't sell in Australia anyway.' (The bastards didn't invite me.)

- 'It was disgraceful. They should be sued for vilification of women. I'm never going to one of their stupid shows again, hideous misogynists.' (It was all bum cheeks, bare breasts and prostitute clothing and I work on a newspaper, so I can say so.)

Beautiful strangers

I once bought a man's entire life in a box. I thought it was just a box of old maps which would be great for wrapping presents, but when I got it home and looked at it all I realised it was a time capsule.

There was a complete set of 1930s London Transport leisure maps, with beautifully illustrated covers, showing all the lovely places at the end of the tube lines where you could go rambling. I can imagine those rambles in stout shoes and a tweed jacket, through copper beeches and mighty oaks, conkers on the ground. And then a pint of beer in an old Surrey pub.

I hope Mr Map enjoyed those simple pleasures because further down in the box there was a large number of army maps of northern France. I have looked at those maps many times trying to picture the landscape they helped

Mr Map to navigate. Or perhaps he was Captain Map at that point.

I've never been sure if I was looking at the battlefields of Flanders, or the Normandy landings, but whichever war it was, Captain Map survived it. There were lots of maps from his travels, including a trip to South Africa in the early 1930s. The first-class passenger list from the ship is in there, in elegant Art Deco typography. I can see them on that voyage. Just like the one in *Brideshead Revisited*. I have always wondered whether there were any love affairs at sea. In white linen. Whatever he got up to in Africa, Mr Map travelled extensively in the United States, by car, in the 1950s, and he went back to England eventually (1960s Ordnance Survey maps).

I had forgotten about Mr Map until today when I went into one of those shops that re-sells designer clothing, and met Madame Hermès. Well, I didn't meet her exactly, I met her clothes. You don't often find gear by Hermès in those shops (and believe me, I'm looking), it's so expensive and such good quality it tends to be last-a-lifetime stuff, so I was instantly intrigued.

The first things I noticed were some enamel bangles in a locked display case. Then I saw there were about four Hermès scarves in there, too, and six Hermès cashmere jumpers. Mint condition, signature gold buttons at the neck. Hardly worn, no pilling, not even under the arms.

Black, navy, grey, cream and two green. I know how Howard Carter felt when he discovered Tutankhamen's tomb.

But as always tomb robbers had got there first – the Kelly bag had already gone. For $800. I could have wept, but rallied when I heard it was green. That really started me thinking. If you can only have one Kelly bag in your life it's never going to be a green one. You'll have a black one, then a camel, then you might move into interesting skins, but a green one is going to be low on the list. Who was this woman? Why did she like green so much? And what else was she throwing out? I picked that shop over like a vulture.

Next find was a beautiful grey flannel skirt, with two zip pockets on the back edged with leather. Gorgeous with that grey sweater. And then something very special – a dark red coat of a style that is correctly called a redingote, nipped in at a high waist, sweeping out to the ankle, large flaps on the pockets, very Scarlet Pimpernel. The kind of coat you would wear to sweep through the Palais Royal in November, in long boots. Carrying a green Kelly bag.

And while you might look like a poet in that coat, you just might be on your way for a bikini wax, because the last thing I found was definitely intended for serious poolside action. It was a mint green towelling beach playsuit. Not the kind of thing you'd throw on for a Bondi dip. More like Cap Ferrat.

Oh Madame Hermès, I wonder who you are and why you are selling your things. But whatever the reason, thank you. I'm going to have that black cashmere jumper for life.

Accidental coutur-ist

The shirt was made from such a brilliant print – a hyper-real photomontage of tropical fish and coral – that it was a few moments before I noticed that the fellow wearing it, standing on the next escalator step up from me at a city railway station, was a rough old diamond in his seventies.

With his two-tone white and yellow hair standing up like a brush, he looked like the kind of gnarly old digger who props up the bar at his local pub, watching the doggies on TV and growling 'Owareyamate?' at all comers. And there he was in a shirt that any Generation Y postmodern ironic Newtown or Brunswick dude would have been stoked to unearth in an op-shop. Or that any South Yarra or Paddington Generation X fashion victim would be thrilled to find copied in a cutting-edge designer boutique.

The shirting equivalent of vinyl wood-grain wallpaper,

it was such an unusually magnificent piece of kitsch that it made me wonder what had gone through Mr Shirt's head as he was getting dressed that morning. Was it, 'I'm going into town, it's a nice day, better wear my best short-sleeved shirt, the one with the fish on it'? Or was it just, 'Where the bleep is my nearest shirt?' Or even, 'Sniff, sniff, this'll do'? But, actually, it looked clean and pressed, so maybe there was a Mrs Shirt there, too, saying, 'Wear your nice fish shirt, Ted, I've ironed it for you specially.'

Then I started pondering what Fish Shirt Man was thinking when he bought that wild garment. Did he choose it because he loved the bright print, because warm tones flatter his colouring, or because he likes tropical fish? Or perhaps it was just the first one he came across the day he went out to get a new shirt because he had spilled too much sauce on his other one. (Someone moved the pie mid-squirt.) For all I know, he went out looking for a tropical fish shirt, or had it specially made, because he is the president of the Australian Fish Fanciers Association and he was off to the annual general meeting. Maybe he was wearing it as a dare. Or to advertise fish food. I'll never know, dammit.

Why ever he has it, I actually loved Fish Shirt Man's mad fish shirt, but I'm sure it wasn't for the same reasons that he does – and that's something I obsess about whenever I see little old ladies (or tall old ladies, for that matter) carrying copies of Prada bags. Do they know their handbag is a plausible copy of Miuccia Prada's latest style and hope that people will think it is the real thing, in the same way that impoverished young fashion assistants will score a $20 Canal Street version just to have the look? Or did they just happen to like it when they saw it in a shop? Or was it the only black one under $50?

In short, I am fascinated by how sane people – that is, those not formally involved in fashion – come to be wearing the clothes they do, because for those of us inextricably caught up in the madness of haute couture and the rest of it, even the smallest clothing purchase is a major life decision. You don't just grab a generic item with the lack of discretion Homer Simpson applies to food (cookie, mouth). Everything you choose is a semiotic satellite dish of who you are, who you think you are, and who you wish you were. You wear your heart, your hopes and your bank balance on your sleeve (and your shoe and your handbag).

So while I am often scruffy, sometimes daggy and occasionally downright slobby, I just can't imagine being accidentally dressed. And I wouldn't mind a tropical-fish-print shirt, either.

GSOH

I know I am absolutely the last person on earth to get on to this, but I have just fallen very much in love with Ricky Martin.

I'd heard about him of course – was sick to death of hearing about him, actually, and how I'd missed out by not seeing him live when he was in Sydney. But I really couldn't see what all the fuss was about.

I'd heard his pappy Latino music and couldn't be bothered with it, and I'd seen pictures of him, but so what? A good-looking dark-skinned man with great abs. You see a million of those down on Bondi Beach any sunny Sunday, so why all the fuss?

Well, last night I saw the video clip for his song 'She Bangs', and one look at his eyes and I totally got it. Not only is Ricky – sigh – terribly good-looking with a great bod, he's got a GSOH. A good sense of humour. You can see it in his eyes.

In the video clip all these beautiful women with practically no clothes on are writhing around all over him and his shirt's coming off (oh God). In the middle of it all he looks straight at the camera (or maybe it was straight at *me*) with an expression that seems to say, 'Struth, mate, they'll have my fillings out in a minute.'

What Ricky has is a very distinct twinkle. A twinkle that tells you immediately he is the kind of person you could have really good church giggles with at inappropriate moments. And because of the GSOH twinkle I'm now mad about him, like the rest of the world.

But forget a romantic dinner on a Saint Tropez terrace, I would love to go on a camping holiday with him. You'd be hysterical over the groundsheet before you'd even left your own street. He'd do funny things with the tent pegs, you can just see it in him.

It's exactly the same kind of twinkle that made craggy old Paul Hogan an international star. Let's face it, Croc Dundee was not that hot to look at (and we won't go into his recent plastic surgery any more than we shall be discussing Ricky's sexuality), but that cheeky knowing look in his eye made him terribly attractive.

Sometimes you meet elderly taxi drivers and septagenarian fruit sellers who have the same twinkle. Some children have it and some dogs. It's a kind of complicity – we're in this together and we're going to have a laugh about it. It's the most attractive thing on earth.

Then you meet the opposite type, the beautiful person with absolutely NSOH. I never know what to do with myself when I come across them – and there is a disconcertingly large number of them at large.

I just don't know how to interact with people who are not in a state of constant alert for something amusing, and I find it deeply distressing when I meet one. It's as though they don't wish to engage with you at all, because a laugh or a smile about the silliest little thing is an instant bond between humans. Dogs sniff each other's bottoms, we have a bit of a laugh – it's how we diffuse the tension between strangers. People who don't understand that repel me.

For all his golden skin, floppy hair, Ninja turtle tummy and lithe thighs, if Ricky (RICKY!!!) had been po-faced about the lissome luvlies who were sexually harassing him in that video, I wouldn't have fancied him at all, but he clearly thought it was the funniest thing ever. And that is why I would fly to Taipei to see him if he were playing there tonight.

So next time you're feeling as sexy as a sack of turnips, stop obsessing about how imperfect you are and think of something funny. If you've got a twinkle in your eye, you're the most gorgeous thing going.

Hairdos and don'ts

Have you noticed how people don't really have hairstyles any more? After undertaking my usual in-depth research on the topic (watching people go by in Pitt Street Mall), I have concluded that there are three styles of hair for women these days: long and unlayered, medium and layered, and short and layered. The only other differentials are fringe/no fringe and straight/curly. They are really just generic hair, not hairstyles, or hairdos. And none of them have names.

But not so long ago it was all about getting a particular haircut – and they all had names. It was key. You'd go in and say you wanted a 'Purdey', a 'Shag', a 'Bowie', a 'Wedge', a 'Mary Quant', an 'Eton crop' or – one I was obsessed with – a 'Coupe Sauvage' (it was a looser shag, invented in Paris where they know all about shagging, let's face it).

Now you just go to the hairdresser praying that you

will come out looking as if you haven't had a haircut. You want to look exactly the same, but better.

Back in the days when haircuts were haircuts and had proper names, they carried tremendous weight. Starting with shingled hair in the 1920s and proceeding in a direct line through long hair for men in the 1960s, and skinhead cuts and Afros in the 70s, your hair was a potent statement about who you were, which tribal group you belonged to and what your values were. A person's haircut was a fairly reliable indicator of how they would vote.

Landmark haircuts were also a big part of growing up. My first rite of passage hairdo happened by accident when I was thirteen. For some reason (probably something ghastly to do with hormones), a lot of my hair fell out. I didn't go bald, it just got thinner and when it grew back I gradually had two distinct lengths of hair all over my head. I didn't really think about it until one of the tough girls at school said to me: 'Have you had a Feather Cut?'

I lied and said I had, because this immediately gained me approval from her tribe – the glamorous fast set who smoked and chewed gum and had electrician boyfriends who hitched up to Wigan Casino at weekends to dance to Northern Soul and take amphetamines. Ace.

When the new layer of hair grew long, I went back to my usual straight, middle-parting thing, and that was the look I had at sixteen when the next landmark haircut took place. After hearing 'Anarchy in the UK' for the first time and studying pictures of the Sex Pistols in *New Musical Express*, I had my Eagles fan hair chopped off into a spiky punk rock crop. I looked pretty vacant and I loved it.

Everywhere I went my hair marked me as a true punk. I made friends with total strangers in the street because it was clear from our hair that we belonged to the same tribe. We also shared our contempt for weekend punks – the ones at a Clash gig in all the right T-shirts and pants, who still had long hair. They didn't show the commitment to have their hair chopped and they weren't the real thing. We gobbed on them.

Now haircuts have lost their meaning, they're just personal style statements. You see guys in the street with a Mohawk and no-one gives them a second look. Likewise, the Skinhead – a Number One – used to be a frightening signal of right-wing politics and a violent disposition. Now every balding man I know has one. My boss has one.

The only haircut left with any sinister semiotic power is the Mullet. That's a style that still says: I'm outside all of society's norms and happy about it. I'd avoid taking a seat next to a Mullet on the train. And if you see an entire family of them, run for it.

I rather miss the badging quality of old-style haircuts but, speaking for myself, the one advantage of not having a particular hair do, is you are less likely to get a hair don't.

Laundry mates

Have just had the most satisfactory conversation. So much common ground, exchanged points of view and cunning tips gratefully gleaned that I can hardly wait to put into practice. You know the kind of conversation where no-one interrupts, no-one disagrees and you just keep looking around at each other like happy dogs, because you're so pleased you've met other people as nuts as you are. The subject? The hierarchy of hand washing.

Ruth, Helen and I spent a good thirty minutes discussing this topic to great mutual enjoyment. We're not exactly the types you'd expect to see nodding at soap powder ads and making mental notes to look out for polyenzymic, low-foaming suds next time we're in aisle one, but entirely by accident we discovered a mutual passion for laundry.

It started out as a discussion of the superiority of agnès b. knitted cotton tops over all others and the surprise revelation that we all shared a ranking system for washing them, whereby middle-aged tops would be thrown in the washing machine (on cold, mind) and even tumble dried, while a Best New Top would be hand washed, rolled in a towel to remove excess moisture and then laid flat to dry – on a fresh towel – like a crusader's tomb.

Then there were subcategories of worn in, but not out, items that would be machine washed and spun, then removed for flat drying, in an attempt to arrest decay. Another stratum of slightly newer ones might be hand washed, *spun*, then flat dried.

Ruth told a sad tale of a very old top on which she had inflicted several years of brutal mechanical washing and drying, before realising that it was the best top she had ever found, which had deserved the five-star hand treatment all along. Although it has long been charcoal rather than your true black and is fast approaching transparency, she reckons she has wrung – sorry, sponged and rolled – a few more years out of it by returning it to the laundry A list.

Having established perfect communion on this topic we then moved on to more general wash-day matters. There was an earnest comparison of top loader versus front loader washers. The 'you've had enough, out you come' and 'in goes the dropped sock' advantage of the top loader was beyond dispute, but we were in total consensus that the round and round wheel motion of the front loader was far superior, in terms of clothes care, to the brutal churning action of the top loader. There was also the question of the water bill, which could be dramatically reduced with a front loader, although the direct chucking of powder into the top loader's drum for pre-wash dissolving appealed to us all enormously, compared to the messy powder drawer.

On the subject of drying there was more variety of views. Helen favours the fluffing effect of tumble drying towels, while Ruth reckons you end up with half your Fieldcrest pile in the filter, drastically shortening towel life span. She also made a claim for the loofah effect of the board-like line-dried towel, which was not entirely convincing.

The next area was ironing: do you? Margaret (that's me) is entirely of the iron everything, or better still pay someone else to do it, school and cannot sleep on sheets which have not felt the kiss of the steam iron, or put out monogrammed hand towels which haven't been blessed with a little starch. An unironed tea towel is to her a thing of horror.

But Ruth and Helen rejoined that if you know your pegging, line drying can negate the need to iron. The secret is in the full-tension pegging action at very specific non-marking points. For non-perfect drying days, both have developed a system of rigorous pegging on indoor clothes airers which produces the same results. A top tip.

The only area we didn't get onto was preferred brands of wool wash, pre-soakers, general detergents, fabric conditioners and the new glamour lavender rinses. Dammit. Wonder when they're free for tea.

House musing

Your house is not a handbag. Just thought I'd mention that as people seem to be confusing homes with fashion accessories these days. You know, something you change every couple of months when you feel like a little bit of a lift. As in, I'm feeling a bit flat. I know! I'll redecorate the entire house. That's better. Now where did I put that credit card . . .

It is true, of course, that just like your clothes, where you live is a very clear reflection of who you are, who you think you are and how you feel about all that. People who let piles of old newspapers form into snow drifts and never clean the grouting in the bathroom probably have levels of self-esteem best expressed by twenty-four-hour Kmart trackie daks. While those who have gold-plated plaster lions at their gate are liable to be fond of a spot of Versace before breakfast.

But it's not as simple as that. Depending on the angle of the moon (and the consequent angle of my stomach) I might, from one day to the next, feel only up to shuffling around the house in foul trackpants and unwashed hair, while the very next morning, I might feel like sliding into something Liz Hurley would consider racy and heading for Panthers of Penrith. This doesn't mean I am going to redecorate from trailer park to Miami mansion to go with it. My house is somewhere in the middle and goes with all my outfits.

We never were supposed to change the look of our houses to reflect every little shift of mood. Apart from keeping the rain off, that is what clothes are for. You can take them on and off all on your own, without waiting for a tradesman to come and do it for you. So from nine till five you can be a cool and collected corporate chick in a neat little suit and a dazzlingly white T-shirt and after six you can re-emerge as Fifi la Jolie Bon Bon in a flowery skirt, a tight cardigan and strappy sandals. Or, if you're a bloke, be Dylan McDermott on Friday and Marilyn Manson on Saturday.

The whole fabulous fun of clothes is that we can use them to showcase all the fascinating little facets of our personalities. This is not the point of houses. Your home is meant to represent the solid, stable part of your life, yet we are under increasing pressure to switch from Martha

Stewart beach house to Dr No helipad at the drop of an interiors magazine.

You know why, of course. They want our money. Now that they've fooled us all into buying more clothes than we can possibly ever wear out, it is no coincidence that the big fashion designers like Ralph Lauren, Calvin Klein and Donna Karan are moving heavily into homewares. Witchery is doing cushions and candles, for heaven's sake. And because fashion houses are used to changing from Mongolian Warrior Woman to Lost In Space from one season to the next, it should be no surprise that they are trying to get us to take the same attitude with our home decor.

The terrible thing is that you can get sucked in without meaning to, because just as with clothes, whatever is now decreed the 'new' interiors look is flogged to such a degree and copied so mercilessly down the retail food chain that you become sick of it before you've even paid for it. If I see another celadon plate (with matching team and tone chopstick rest), or anything made of bamboo, I will spew interestingly textured beige and dark brown vomit all over it.

Some people are even making the equivalent of fashion-based plastic surgery decisions, entirely renovating dear little terrace houses to rubble and rebuilding them so they resemble recently scrubbed operating theatres. That house might make it into *Belle*, but in ten years' time I reckon it is going to look as dated as 1970s sauna-style pine cladding or 80s chintz swagging does now. And it will be even more tiresome and expensive to put right than Pamela Anderson's boob job.

They'd do much better just to buy a new handbag and get over it.

Elegance lost

I know where the Dutch artist Bosch got the inspiration for his gruesome paintings of sinners writhing in hell. He went to a Gucci sample sale. 'Up to 80 per cent off!!' screamed the posters. 'We must clear our warehouse!' And we must have all the stuff in it, we agreed, and ran into Sydney Town Hall like a plague of rabid rats with credit cards.

The scenes within displayed human nature in all its raw ugliness. Heaving crushes of bodies clawing at piles of wallets and key pouches. Racks of innocent clothes being ruthlessly raped and pillaged. High-status handbags tossed around like footballs, and scrums of tiny women shouldering through tightly packed crowds with a level of aggression the most fearsome rugby prop would run away from. Harsh cries of 'That's mine!' as someone else dares to touch a viciously won prize. Mothers using strollers as deadly weapons. Tiny toddlers left to be trampled by a herd with the scent of polished calf in its nostrils.

All this in the pursuit of elegance.

I was lucky: without committing too much GBH on anyone, I garnered a pair of suede ankle boots with foxy little heels and toes so sharp you could drill teeth with them; the kind of thing Chrissie Hynde would wear to pick up the kids from school. They would have started life around $900 and they were mine for $190. Bargain! Then I found a lovely pair of all-leather slip-ons for my significant other. $220, down from around $800. Cheeeap. Gimme. Gimme more. I want more. More bigger now quick. Faster pussycat kill kill.

That was when sanity departed. Dragging my booty behind me in the standard issue polythene sack, I was round that room like a Viking recently landed in York. My elbows flailing like Boadicea's deadly wheels, I charged through rails of ready to wear and off again, hacking down all before me until I reached the ultimate challenge – small leather goods.

For some reason this slag heap of well-fingered purses, credit card holders, make-up bags and wallets, long since parted from their boxes, was the focus for the fiercest hand to hand combat. One woman was particularly shameless: heavily pregnant, she barged her way between fellow scavengers with a bump of her lump, taking advantage of their surprise to insert her grasping hand like the mechanical grabber in one of those pick-a-toy fairground attractions.

Suddenly it was all too much. A swathe of handsome silk ties and scarves was beckoning but, battle weary, I went to pay. The queue for the tills went right around the room, nearly meeting itself coming back. I stood in it for ten minutes before sense began to seep back.

In a quiet corner (nothing for sale) I took the boots out of the bag and had another look. They were gorgeous. They were a bargain. They were not worth standing in a queue for an hour for, surrounded by people behaving like they were auditioning for Quentin Tarantino. I put them – and the slip-ons – back and left.

I'm still a bit sad about those boots, but the disco inferno in Sydney Town Hall taught me something about designer shopping. What you actually go home with is only part of it. The process is as important as the product. What you are paying for (apart from the name and superior styling) is the experience of going into one of those swishy snooty boutiques, being served with some respect (possibly sitting down) and coming out with a stonking great carrier bag which, for the remainder of your shopping day, acts like a passport into all the other shops you are normally too shy to enter.

That is all part of the magic of paying too much for designer accessories. A rematch between Mohammed Ali and George Foreman is not. Even at half the price.

Bad buys

First you have to find clothes you like, that also happen to suit you. Then you have to find your size in the right colour. Worst of all, you have to pay for them. But the trials of fashion don't end even with the horror of the credit card statement. Here are Forty-six Things That Can Go Wrong With Clothing Purchases.

1 The shop had a skinny mirror.
2 The fabric picks up every bit of fluff in the universe.
3 The fabric goes bobbly after two wears.
4 Even after you've had the trousers narrowed, the waist let out and the collar altered, it's still horrible and still doesn't suit you.
5 It's so creased after one hour of wearing that you look as if you've been wrapped by Christo.

6   You've 'invested' in the real thing and two days later every rip-off shop in Australia has an adequate version in the window.

7   You've bought the rip-off version. So has everyone else.

8   You've invested in the real thing and two months later it looks so two months ago.

9   You never quite get round to dyeing it.

10 Dry clean only.

11 You don't – only to find they meant it.

12 Somehow you never do lose those five kilos.

13 It's purple.

14 As you take it from the spinner, you see that the arms resemble the tentacles of a giant squid.

15 It doesn't go with anything you own. Even the things you bought specially to go with it.

16 It's almost what you were looking for.

17 It looked amazing on your more attractive friend.

18 It's a yellow suit.

19 It's made of cream silk and you drop half your lunchtime laksa on it.

20 You hand wash it. It was made of crepe.

21 You've had the sleeves/legs shortened half a centimetre too much.

22 It's itchy.

23 It's hot.

24 It's full of static.

25 It's see-through (and not in a good way).

26 It sticks where it hits.

27 It makes you sweatier than Pat Rafter on a hot day.

28 You have to iron it.

29 You bought it in London in February and the last time it got cold enough to wear it here was in 1853.

30 You bought it in Paris when you were feeling bohemian.

31 You bought it in Goa.

32 You bought it on a freak thin day after a severe stomach upset.

33 You bought it two days before menstruation.

34 You bought it the day after having the best sex of your life.

35 You were still drunk.

36 After one wearing, the trousers have bigger knees than Mike Tyson.

37 You have it dry cleaned at [insert own hated clothes-destroyer dry cleaners].

38 You bought it because it has a designer label and was 50 per cent off.

39 You bought it because it was cheap and cheerful. It's just cheap.

40 Your two-year-old bursts into tears when he sees you in it.

41 Your mother bursts into tears when she sees
    you in it.

42 Your partner goes quiet when he sees you in it.

43 Your best friend laughs hysterically when she sees
    you in it.

44 You see yourself in a shop window. And do all of
    the above.

45 Someone at a party comments on your 'interesting'
    dress.

46 A kindly bus driver asks when you are due.

Watertight solutions

There are two conditions that make achieving a sense of glamour impossible: head colds and rain. A running nose, red scaly nostrils and a brain full of porridge render any amount of personal grooming redundant, although I'm never sure if you look as bad as you feel when you have a vicious case of the snotters. It's like wearing a mucous helmet that cuts you off from the world and distorts all perception.

Heavy rain just makes you feel like a hobbit.

It's impossible to walk tall and stride out when stair rods of cold water are coming randomly down your neck and people at street crossings are giving you impromptu retinal surgery with their umbrella spokes.

The only thing that makes a day of falling water bearable is the prospect of the sofa, the quilt, cable television featuring Gregory Peck, and lashings of hot chocolate. So what are you supposed to wear when it's pouring with rain, but it's hot? A bikini?

It's the one sartorial brainteaser harder than smart casual, but I do know who I don't want to look like – the man I saw at the station this morning who was wearing a long plastic rain mac over shorts and reef sandals.

Still, he may not be as mad as he looked; open shoes are quite a cunning solution for the hot rain dilemma, as the water can go straight through and out the back. And at least you can dry wet feet and start again – an office redolent of steaming wet socks can be a very bad start to your week.

Working on this principle, on hot rain days I tend to wear my black rubber Spice Girl shoes, which are like beach slides atop 10-centimetre platforms, in the hope they will work like seventeenth-century pattens and elevate me above the mud and swirling drainwater. You do have to be a bit careful on slippery surfaces, however, because it's a long way to fall. As Geri Halliwell will tell you.

But for cooler days, at least one pair of closed rain shoes is an essential in any wardrobe. Not just tragic old trainers you don't mind sloshing through puddles in, but a pair of shoes that look decent enough to wear to work and don't let the deluge in. The key is integral rubber soles. Those stick-on ones I sometimes ruin good leather-soled shoes with, out of some misguided notion of practicality, just don't do it. In fact, they seem to seal the wet into the leather and keep it there.

On a wet day your outfit will always start with your rain shoes – and it should end with a raincoat that you don't loathe. It's bad enough that the weather is foul without looking like Columbo (the crumpled crimebuster) on top. So it's really worth investing in a decent raincoat – ideally one that keeps out the rain. Beware the word 'showerproof'. You're not going to be wearing it in the shower. A bloody great tropical downpour demands serious protection – but that doesn't mean you should have to wear something totally at odds with the rest of your life (i.e. a drover's coat or Annapurna parka if you live in the inner city).

But I do warn you that the pursuit of such a coat can take on the Arthurian dimension of the quest for the comf-elegant work shoe. I finally found my dream coat in Prada last year, but still wake whimpering in the night after a dream about how much I paid for it . . .

And my last tip for surviving the rainy season: buy the nastiest umbrella you can find. That way, you are guaranteed never to lose it.

The real thing

One of the most interesting fashion shows I ever saw in Paris didn't involve any designer clothes. It was the rehearsal for a Chanel parade, held several hours before the show was due to begin, with Karl Lagerfeld and his right-hander, Lady Amanda Harlech, watching in earnest concentration. (I was just there perving.)

The models, about sixty of them and none of them 'names', trooped along the runway in their own clothes. Quite a few were smoking, most were wearing very scruffy jeans (in the then new 'dirty' denim) and one of them was carrying a small dog. Most of them wore sandshoes of great decrepitude, several were barefoot and the only one in a pair of shiny high heels stuck out like an air hostess in a mosh pit. It was fascinating.

Because they were all about the same height and thinness

(180 centimetres, size 8), they didn't stand out the way models do when they move among normal earthlings. In fact, they just looked like a big gaggle of skinny schoolgirls on a geology field trip. With no make-up, their hair greasy and lank from three weeks of being tortured into high-concept fashion-show 'looks', it was hard even to perceive them as particularly pretty, let alone beautiful. There was certainly nothing 'super' about them.

What a contrast to a memory of ten years ago, when I saw Linda Evangelista outside the Louvre, after a Chanel show funnily enough, jumping onto the back of a Vespa in a red Chanel suit and high heels. She knew how good she looked as the handsome courier ferried her off to the next booking in her packed schedule and, as they zipped into the traffic, she threw back her head and laughed.

The rest of us just gawped, looking around for the American *Vogue* camera crew, but it was no shoot – it was real life as lived by the most super of the supermodels at the height of the supermodel era.

That moment is now well and truly over, and the girls at the Chanel rehearsal looked as if they would be catch-ing the bus to their next show (unlikely, actually). But while they didn't have Linda's Eva Perón charisma, they did have something far more interesting – reality. Real people are the most fascinating thing in the world, much more interesting than models (unless you're one of the sad 'modeliser' men in 'Sex and the City').

Of course, all the women tramping the catwalk that morning were models by profession – but before the depersonalising application of highly stylised make-up and hairdos, they were still discernible as real women. A fashion show is all about imposing a unified look on a bunch of disparate individuals to express the designer's vision for the collection. But while they were dressed in their own clothes, you could still determine different personalities – this one a little sulky, this one flashing cheeky looks at Kaiser Karl, another looking vague and fey.

Some of them just plonked along, bored to death; others practically trotted round, clearly eager to get back to the book, the CD or the gossip they had been caught up in backstage before the rehearsal call. One or two – including the one in the heels – gave it all they had, walking the walk with head up and hips forward, charisma set to stun, clearly hoping to stand out.

Three hours later, I watched them do it all over again. The same group of tall young women, reborn in wigs and slap to create a master race of expressionless replicants, with funny walks. I loved the clothes in that fashion show (especially the classic Chanel tweed jacket reincarnated as a zip-front coat), but I preferred the women as themselves.

Martha knows best

Do you shine your shoes? Do you give your jacket a once-over with a clothes brush before you leave the house? Do you put things with missing buttons in the mending basket and not back into the wardrobe? Do you let suits air for twenty-four hours after they've been in a smoky environment?

I ask these questions because you do see a lot of 'smart' executive types walking around the CBD wearing the thirstiest little shoes and with great drifts of scurf on their shoulders. And in crowded lifts, other people's jackets sometimes smell like bedsits. Which makes you wonder whether, under all that tailoring, they perform even the most perfunctory acts of daily self-grooming.

But while I do think shoe polish has a place in every life, I have also come to believe it is possible to be too well groomed. This thought seized me when I watched Martha Stewart address the Magazine Publishers of Australia conference in Sydney.

For those of you who are not already slaves to Martha the Magnificent (I got her autograph . . .), she is a US phenomenon – the publisher of lifestyle bible *Martha Stewart Living*, a home, gardening and food magazine of such exquisite taste that it has defined a new style of comfy elegance and changed the way Americans live. (And if you come around to my house for dinner and there is a place card made from an autumn leaf and a centrepiece fashioned from acorn-shaped cinnamon cookies and red-sprayed twigs, you will see how much impact she has had on my life.)

Martha Stewart Living has also – along with associated web sites, books, mail order, TV shows and licensing deals – made Martha a billionaire. And there she was, taking the stage in a simple grey trouser suit and very sensible flat shoes. Her hair was a bit mussed up. The only indication that she is one of the most powerful women in the USA was a pair of diamond earstuds the size of Minties.

What a contrast between her and many of the ambitious young women in the audience, so assiduously groomed and done up in their dress-for-success outfits, 2000-style.

In the 1980s, when 'power dressing' for women was

invented, it meant desexualising skirt suits that were the female equivalent of the male business suit, with pussy-cat-bow blouses that were the equivalent of the shirt and tie. Margaret Thatcher made it her uniform. Well, it worked for her, didn't it? The idea was that to succeed in a man's world you had to neutralise the sexual messages inherent in women's clothing, without getting into full Marlene Dietrich drag. You wanted your clothes to make your body disappear so that your brain could dominate proceedings.

But the young women worshipping at the shrine of Saint Martha clearly had a different agenda. I watched two of them clip-clopping to the auditorium in high-heeled mules, and sleek jersey skirts and cardigans which showed off gym-toned bodies. Their hair was perfectly blow-dried and their nails recently manicured. They were tastefully made up, their jewellery was discreet and they smelled nice. In short: they were shiny, sexy babes and it really struck me how different a message they were sending out compared to their corporate ancestors of twenty years ago. Not so much takin' care of business as taking care of me first.

Their post-feminist agenda seems to be: just look at me – I find time to do aerobics, go to the beauty salon, mix and match expensive separates, have my hair done, accessorise, stretch, floss, do positive affirmations and get to this conference on time. If I can do all this for myself, just imagine what I can do for you . . .

I'm not sure about this message. They looked a bit Marketing Executive Barbie to me. But then, Margaret Thatcher always wore high heels.

Sales pitch

On my current voyage around world retail, it has become clear that some people have no idea how to shop. Not what to buy – that's the easy bit – but how to behave. There is a certain etiquette to shopping, and people who don't observe it are in the same category as those who wear white to weddings, talk with their mouths full or pour wine into their own glasses before those of fellow diners. Like all good manners, shopping rules derive from basic consideration for others, so that everyone can enjoy a fair go at the purple ostrich ankle-strap high heels and fine cashmere polonecks. (Get off, that's mine!)

The Gucci and Prada stores in Milan are mobbed during fashion week by rabid fashion editors foaming at the mouth, furious locals, pushy Germans, loud Americans and hordes of young Japanese tourists who are obliged by custom to buy a designer present for everyone they know. So instead of a divine shopping experience that makes you feel like a brand-name heiress, these fashion temples resemble David Jones's sock department on the first day of the sales.

Bad behaviour I have witnessed includes covering glass display cases with coats so no-one else can see what's inside; snatching up one of the bags another shopper is in the process of auditioning and posing with it in front of the mirror; hanging around the middle of a shop in gormless groups and getting in everyone's way; helping yourself to items off the shelves behind the counter; interrupting high-level consultations between shopper and salesperson to bark 'Have you got these in 38?'; reaching past a fellow browser to snatch a tasty item; and elbowing someone out of the way to get at something on a rack.

But the most interesting shopping ineptitude I have seen took place in an expensive children's-wear shop in Belgravia, London's most elegant quarter. As I entered the establishment with my friend Josephine, two baby strollers completely blocked our way, while Dad and the kids lounged on the ottoman and Mum walked around pointing at things she wanted. The little ones, both under four, were dressed like Spanish royal children circa 1960, the boy in a pintucked romper suit, the girl in a white princess coat and pink patent party shoes. She wore diamond studs in her pierced ears. She may have been three.

The parents, on the other hand, were downright ordinary – not trashy or scruffy, but just not chic or distinguished in any way, except for the huge gold and diamond watch on the man's wrist. And while the mother picked out goodies, he took a Harrods bag from under the buggy and chucked a Steiff collector's edition teddy bear at each toddler, who threw them onto the floor, where they stayed.

I was gripped. All my horrible British class system zoning instincts kicked in. Who were they and where did the dough come from?

He didn't look flashy enough for a bank robber and his wife wasn't wearing enough make-up. Neither of them seemed nerdy or bright enough to be Internet entrepreneurs. She definitely wasn't one of the Spice Girls, so perhaps he was a foreign-currency dealer in the City? But when he opened his wallet to pay for the huge pile of kiddy couture, he didn't have any gold credit cards, so that was out.

As we left the shop, I raised a questioning eyebrow at Josephine to see if she had a handle on it. 'Lottery winners,' she said decisively. And I'm sure she was right. They clearly had tons of money but, while they had sussed out where to find really nice things, they still didn't quite know how to buy them. We resolved at once to start a consultancy firm for the newly rich: Maggie and Jo's How To Spend It.

Get wiggy with it

Never underestimate the power of a wig. I don't mean the power of a ginger wig, like the one worn by the caretaker at my school, to render thirteen-year-old girls senseless with giggles. But the dizzying power of glamour wigs. Drag queens – and Dolly Parton – really know what they're doing when they pop a flaxen mane of silken curls, or flaming locks of auburn hair on top of their ordinary little mousey heads. Bingo! Instant charisma. Anyone can be Jolene in the right wig.

This was brought home to me with force at a wig party I recently attended. First there was the thrill of walking in and not recognising people I work with every day. Then there was the added bonus of suddenly finding many of them keenly sexually attractive, simply because of the addition of a mop of fake hair. And I must confess it is not the first time I have felt strongly attracted to close gay friends once they have popped a rock star wig atop their normally shorn scalps. Every man is Jon Bon Jovi in a shaggy wig. Shaggy's the name and shaggy's the game.

On another wig-inspired occasion I followed a total stranger around a party all night because I was so love-struck by his blond shag wig – although the powder blue polyester suit, platform shoes and 100 per cent nylon frill-front dress shirt had something to do with it, too. He looked like the blond one from Sweet at Noddy Holder's wedding. Any man who would go out in public like that for a laugh was the one for me, I thought. Especially if he kept it all on in bed. Sadly our relationship never got beyond one ecstatic boogie to 'Ballroom Blitz', when he took his wig off for a breather and my ardour died in an instant. He suddenly looked so – ordinary.

Wigs make you extraordinary. They make you bigger. Literally. With a Marge Simpson, an Ab Fab Patsy, the full Priscilla Presley, or an early Michael Jackson, you obviously take up more physical space, but somehow you take up more psychic space as well. On my most recent wig outing I went your Jacqueline Susanne route, rendered brilliantly by my hairdressser (thanks, Andrea), with the help of a very long blonde switch, half a can of hairspray and a photo-graph from a recent Versace show.

Thanks to the sheer height of my fiercely back-combed

do, plus the major stacks it demanded I wear, I was a good half-metre taller. All that combined with a pair of op-shop TV screen sunnies and my vintage fake leopard coat, a devastating combo I would normally feel far too shy to wear together, I felt like a fearless ultra-femme. I strutted into that party. And I wasn't the only one living it large in fake hair.

Entering that room full of people in show wigs was like suddenly being jacked into an episode of 'The Simpsons'. Everyone's personality was written boldly upon their heads and, far from making them feel shy and exposed, it seemed to free the spirit. The few people at that party not wearing hired hair looked colourless and sad, like little brown sparrows in a cage full of parrots. Parrots doing the funky chicken, at that.

So if you've got a problem with self-esteem, feel like a walking charisma vacuum and reckon porridge has more personality than you at a party, forget Prozac, gurus, group therapy and even tequila slammers. What you need is a big wig. The world's a whole lot sweeter viewed from beneath an acrylic thatch. Just ask Dolly.

Crashing symbols

Hear ye, hear ye: we abandon the time-honoured symbols of clothing at our peril. Be afeared of a world where a man's robe speaks no more to his fellow man than the wind speaks to the boughs of the trees, for he shall be as the beast in the wilderness, and chaos and anarchy will surely reign among us. Shelter your children from this world of fashion falsehood where raiment holds no truth and there is no honour in finery.

In other words: the end of the world is nigh because no-one wears their uniform any more.

Previously I have written about the confusion that can be caused at work by the current trend to abandon corporate dress codes. I might not, for example, have yelled, 'And who the hell are you?' at the man who barged rudely into a private meeting the other week had he been dressed in a suit and tie rather than shorts and combat boots. That would have been an indication that he had an important executive role within the corporate hierarchy and wasn't the itinerant sandwich seller he resembled.

While that might reveal dodgy values on my part (actually I have nothing against sandwich sellers), it would have saved embarrassment all round (especially for me, still blushing). But really, it was all his fault because he had irresponsibly abandoned the visual language of clothing. In all situations, clothes are a vital form of shorthand, letting us know with one glance exactly what manner of person we are dealing with. Ask any skinhead. Or a passing nun. A High Court judge. A drag queen. Krusty the Clown. The Nanny. The Dalai Lama. Hulk Hogan. John Howard. Liberace.

If clothes weren't such instant and subtle communicators (well, not so subtle in Liberace's case), why would film directors go to such lengths to get the costumes right? A character's clothes are essential indicators for the viewer. But the way the world is going, with newspaper editors, CEOs and hospital doctors all turning up for work in cargo pants, Mambo shirts and deck shoes, soon Mr Spielberg et al. will be able to dispense with the Edith Heads and Luciana Arrighis and just dress everyone in tracksuits, like one of those 1970s productions of *Hamlet* played in the round, with everyone sitting on cardboard boxes.

Consider, also, the complex sartorial semiotics of the armed forces. The whole point of uniforms is (a) to instil a sense of straight-backed itchy-trousered discipline in the wearer and (b) to let everyone know just how scared to be of everyone else. And it makes good sense on a deafening battlefield, doesn't it, to have rank clearly defined from a distance by button, stripe and epaulet? As enemy fire rains down, you can hardly be expected to find out who's in charge by asking your mates, 'Is that bloke in the silverchair tour T-shirt the general? Or is it the one in the flowery frock?' It must also be useful to know which side everyone is on.

There are other ways, lost to us now, in which dress used to be a very handy signalling code. Take mourning attire. The whole notion seems creepily Victorian now – especially as so many of us wear all black as an everyday look. But wouldn't it be helpful to know that the reason the fellow in the bank has just been so snippy with you is that a close relative has recently died (black armband)? You'd gladly give up your seat on a crowded train to that pale-faced lady who has just lost her beloved husband (head-to-toe black). And make an extra effort to smile at the one who lost hers six months ago (head-to-toe purple).

They were called dress codes for a reason.

Hair raising

I'm in a daze. A bad hair daze. What happens? One day my hair is a shiny bouncy happening thing, the next – today – it's having a total gross-out bad hair day. They seem to come from nowhere. I haven't changed my shampoo, my conditioner, my diet, my attitude, or my hair washing and drying routine, but what created a smooth glossy head yesterday has produced a weird dry/greasy/sticky mop today. It feels like a thatched roof sitting on my head. A very old thatched roof. My scalp aches. My hair smells funny. No I haven't got my period, but thanks for asking anyway.

One theory I am considering is that aliens came and did a hair transplant on me in the night. Because this is not my hair. My hair is straight with a slight wave. This hair is not wavy, or kinky, or even frizzy. It's bent. There are bends in it. Where it should fall and bounce and swish, it bends. So I'm having a bad hair day and now I've got an attack of the bends.

Then there are my antennae. These are special bits of hair that stick out of the sides of my head just behind my ears. I could probably pick up Triple J on them if I tried, but nothing – nothing – will make them lie down. The first thing I always do on a bad hair day is scrape the whole lot back into a severe, yet stylish, ponytail, but the antennae always spring from their bindings like greyhounds leaving the starting boxes at Harold Park. And they're off!

I've tried cleaving them to my head with greasy stuff, but it just makes them into pointy greasy antennae. I've tried gluing them back with hairspray, which works for about five minutes and then they just spring out again and are so dry my head is liable to spontaneously combust. I could be my own bush fire.

In a really dire moment, with a black tie dinner to go to in fifteen minutes, I tried cutting them shorter with nail scissors, but then they were just shorter antennae. They could only pick up AM stations. My antennae are so wilful, they even stick out from the edges of a desperation Alice band at a perfect right angle to my head. They're the hair equivalent of a raised middle finger. Faced with my antennae, I have considered taking up

Buddhism in a serious way. Not for inner peace, but to have a good excuse to shave my head.

Maybe it's something to do with astrology, or numerology, because on a bad hair day everything to do with hair is totally jinxed. That time I had to go to the black tie dinner with antennae as my date, I had carefully booked a blow-dry appointment to ensure Jennifer Anniston locks in any circs. But fate conspired with traffic jams and a dress I accidentally had to try on, and I was late for my appointment. Because I was out of town and using a strange salon they wouldn't fit me in, like they would have at my regular rug joint. And forget surgery. If you go for the chop on a bad hair day you'll come out with something even worse. A bad haircut.

I don't know what the answer is. I really have tried everything, including getting right back into the shower and washing the whole damned thing all over again and not leaving the towel wrapped around my head for a moment longer than the normal time – which is exactly how long it takes me to eat a bowl of cereal – before blow-drying. It didn't work. I just ended up with bad hair that was an hour late for work.

Only time heals a bad hair day. You just have to wait until the stars realign into a more tonsorially fortunate conjunction. Or for the traffic lights to change back to green on Mars so the aliens can bring your real hair back.

Sitting pretty

Fashion is a precise science. It may not seem that way with all the airy-fairy talk about divine chiffons and blissful bias cuts and darling little clutch bags and all that, but when you really analyse it, the rights and wrongs of fashion come down to millimetres.

Take shoulders. I am currently obsessed with the exact shape of the shoulders on Helmut Lang's women's suits. I can spot them at fifty paces (so if you're wearing one, this is a good time to start running, because I want your suit, I want it). I don't know what it is about them exactly, but they sit just perfectly at the edge of the shoulder bone, not rounded like those 1980s shoulder boulders that resembled skateboarders' knee protectors, and not too sharp and flashy, but neat and firm like a classic man's suit jacket. To my fevered eye (I must have one, I MUST), they confer instant authority and decorum on the wearer. The shoulders make the suit stand up straight on its own.

In my last attempt to own a Helmut Lang trouser suit, I tried on several that were perfect, except they weren't my size (I considered liposuction). In a frustrated fashion frenzy, I then took the assistant's advice and tried on the shop's own label 'version' of the suit.

Oh, unhappy comparison. Even apart from the nasty fabric and the funny cut around the groin (Gandhi's loincloth), they hadn't got the shoulders right. I really can't define precisely what the difference was, but they weren't the chairman–of–the–board shoulders of my dreams. I tore that jacket off and fled.

The other unmissable shoulder is by Chanel. Once you get your eye in, you can pick the Chanel shoulder (I know this is getting repetitive, but there really isn't another word for it) from an entire field of racegoers, no matter what manner of garment or fabric it is rendered in. It's a very feminine shape that just cups the, er, shoulder and some-how makes the wearer look more svelte and neatly proportioned.

Like the Helmut Lang version, the Chanel shoulder (arm/neck conjoiner?) segues into a very tight armhole and a close-fitting sleeve that can feel like a straitjacket if you spent all of last summer in Witchery T-shirts, but boy, is it worth it. The perfect shoulder and a slender sleeve can take kilos off your middle, add several centimetres to your height and make you feel like an antipodean Bernadette Rendall. No, I know you've never heard of her, but she's the head of PR for Chanel in Paris and the most elegant woman I have ever met, and you do want to feel like her, believe me.

The other detail where millimetres can make the crucial difference between chic and shabby is trouser length. That's why the whole crop pant thing was such a joy, because your trouser leg really could end anywhere between thigh and floor. But please note the past tense in that sentence. Now fashion and the seasons are dictating a return to real trousers.

I've just ruined two beaut pairs I bought in London at the Joseph sale by having them taken up too much. I had become so used to cropping my pantaloons somewhere around the ankle bone, I didn't think it through properly when I dropped them off to the tailor. So my beautiful grey flannel trackpant-style trews, which should be falling in careless folds and trailing the ground beneath my designer trainers, instead look ready for a smart round of golf. I'm puking. Just a few millimetres have made the difference between most favoured trouser status and . . . huh, those things.

The only thing that would make me feel better about it is a Helmut Lang suit.

Animal attraction

Cockroaches need a makeover. They really should do something about those horrible brown outfits. I'm sure they'd have a completely different image if they weren't always decked out in a colour so unfashionable and so strongly associated with faeces. Because I am certain it is entirely due to the unfortunate colour of their coats that I have always strongly suspected that cockroaches consider the area beneath the lavatory seat a smorgasbord of tasty delights. And that's why I get so upset when I find them marching about in my fridge. I'm not sure if they've washed their feet since dinner.

If they were an attractive shade of aqua I wouldn't mind living with them nearly so much. I'd think they brightened the place up. Oh look, a mummy cockroach and lots of little baby cockroaches. Aren't they sweet? Let's give them some biscuits. Instead of – AAAAAH! Cockroaches! YUK!

Where's the spray? Exterminate. Exterminate.

If cockroaches knew how to dress, I wouldn't be turned into a serial killer every time I saw one. They could at least accessorise. Even dung beetles, who actually do make a living from eating poo, are more attractive than cockroaches, which seems terribly unfair.

They should get some of the more attractive insects to give them some styling advice. They could ask yellow and black ladybirds for starters. One of those landed on my car windscreen the other day and I was thrilled. It felt like a blessing. And I adore red and black ladybirds so much I'd like to have one as a pet because they remind me of two of my favourite things of childhood: Ladybird books and Ladybird pyjamas. And they're lucky, too. Apparently it's good luck if one lands on you. They even have their own nursery rhyme. (It's a bit depressing actually, but it shows how famous and popular they are.)

I suppose there is a song about cockroaches – 'La Cucaracha' – but isn't it something ghastly about only having one leg? That's no good at all. So they need a wardrobe makeover and a new theme tune. Something cheerful and life affirming. Then perhaps someone will make a movie about them. Ants aren't that different in shape from cockroaches really, but they aren't yucky because they're not that particular shade of brown. Shudder.

But there really is no reason why cockroaches couldn't

be more attractive, because putting deadly venom aside for a moment, most insects are beautiful. That's why they have regular fashion moments. Dolce & Gabbana went mad about butterflies one season and put them all over their clothes and Prada once had a collection that made a big feature of embroidered bugs. They gave all the top fashion editors a new accessory – a patent leather beetle – to celebrate. British designer Matthew Williamson once went silly over dragonflies and spiderwebs. But nobody ever features cockroaches. Likewise there is an ancient tradition of brooches in the shape of scarab beetles, dragonflies and bees, studded with precious gems, but to my knowledge Tiffany & Co have never made a cockroach brooch. They didn't find any in Cleopatra's tomb, either.

And there are other creatures which could enormously improve their quality of life if they would only employ a fashion consultant. Hyenas have permanent bad hair days. Sharks need serious orthodentistry. Vultures would look better in little toupees (plus they would benefit from a course in the Alexander Technique to improve their posture). Even rats might not be quite so repellent if they had fluffy fur covers on their tails and nice little shoes.

But for the time being cockroaches insist on wearing brown. They are the only living thing I deliberately kill. Just think about that next time someone tells you clothes don't matter. Or that brown is the new black.

A Clutterbug's Life

I am just about to change my whole life. I'm so excited. And it's so easy. According to this fascinating little book I've just been reading, called *Clear Your Clutter And Turn Into Cameron Diaz* (or something like that), all I have to do is chuck out all the old crap in my home and my life will change entirely. It's all to do with feng shui apparently, which is the ancient art of arranging your home (not a Chinese brand of shoes). Whatever it is, I can hardly wait.

All you have to do is get rid of those teetering piles of unread old newspapers, that collection of 'special' carrier bags you have wedged down the side of the kitchen units and all those might-wear-them-to-a-fancy-dress-party-one-day shoes you have shoved under the bed, and the 'energy' will move freely again in your home – and in your

Life. (There are always a lot of Capital Letters in these Books.)

How this seems to work is that all the space that was taken up by pointless old junk will then fill up instead with rolls of used $50 bills and single heterosexual men who look like Johnny Depp, are as funny as Mikey Robbins and make George Soros feel financially insecure.

You can see why I'm excited. According to this book, clearing the clutter without also helps to clear the clutter within. (You can nod at this point and look Wise.) This means that people who have followed the author's advice have spontaneously lost heaps of weight without effort, as well as becoming multi-millionaires in loose change found under discarded keep-fit gadgets.

Inspired by the thrilling case studies in the book (one woman threw out all her clothes bar five items, and a cheque for $15 000 arrived in the post almost immediately; imagine that), I've started de-cluttering already. I must say my bedroom does look better without a leaning tower of shoe boxes next to the bed and I found 10 cents on the street the other day – amazing! It must be working.

The only problem is that every time I open the wardrobe door a big pile of shoe boxes falls out, which is forcing me to realise that clearing my superficial clutter is not enough. I need to get in touch with my Inner Clutter.

Because while it looks pretty organised on the surface,

peep behind any cupboard door in my place and you will find deep clutter. Every drawer is a Bermuda Triangle of tangled tat. Every closet a black hole of cack. Clearing this lot out properly – i.e. actually taking things out the front door, as opposed to just moving it round and round – could be more traumatic. I'll actually have to part with some of it.

And while it is all too easy to make fun of New Agey self-help books, I can see that this book has a point. One of the reasons I never have anything to wear is because I have too many clothes. I've got so much junk I can't see what junk I've got. All my junk's got junk on top of it. And junk on top of that.

So when I'm frantically trying to find something to wear under a neat little suit, I can't find my two strategically purchased thin cotton black suit T-shirts because they are hidden under all the other black T-shirts (of quite the wrong weights), so I think I have lost them. So then I have to take the suit off and start all over again.

The other thing that happens is that while I'm scrabbling around looking for the T-shirts, I come across a divine little top I had completely forgotten I had. But because it was squashed on a hanger underneath two other shirts, I've also forgotten that it has a button missing and a mystery stain on the front. If I had fewer clothes I would be able to see them all – and I'd be able to see what was wrong with them. And I might get to work on time more often.

So I'm going to do it, I'm going to have an enormous chuck out. And I promise to tell you what happens. (Because that means I will really have to do it.)

The big heave-ho

I had tears in my eyes as I said farewell forever. Looking at them one last time, as I remembered all the amazing experiences we had shared, I blew them a kiss, saying, Goodbye old friends and thank you. Then I chucked the whole lot in the charity clothing bin.

I promised I'd do it and I have. I've been through my wardrobe like a bush fire, determined to throw out anything I haven't worn in the last year. And along with irredeemably stained T-shirts, out of style mini skirts, and jeans which I have finally accepted will never actually fit me again, I threw out some real old friends. Garments I have owned for ten years, which have seen me through all manner of clothing crises, but just don't hack it any more.

The hardest to part with was my English Eccentrics baroque-print red silk shirt. I can still remember the day

I bought that shirt – it would have been in February 1990. I was the editor of a fashion magazine at the time, just about to embark once more on the biannual trips to the Milan–Paris–New York fashion shows.

I knew from experience that you always needed an emergency outfit for 'Quasi Modo' days on those trips, because when you are going to be surrounded by the most stylish people on earth, watching the most beautiful women on earth modelling clothes so fashionable you can't even buy them yet, there is no leeway for a clothing crisis. You have to have something you can wear when everything looks terrible – and you are always in a hurry.

And there it was, this bright red silk shirt that fell mercifully to mid thigh, but was made of the most extraordinary printed fabric with cherubs and garlands up the gazoo, so it didn't matter that you were wearing that most desperate of garments: a Big Shirt.

At £300 it was the most expensive single garment I had ever bought and I felt sick with guilt and horror as I walked out of the shop with it. But boy, was that shirt a good investment. On the Cost Per Wear principle I must have got it down to 50p a shot. It never ever let me down.

I wore Shirty to fashion shows with leggings and great shoes (don't snigger – leggings were the thing in 1990; Anna Wintour was wearing them, too). I wore it to smart lunches on hot days with a neat little skirt and great sandals, and to dinner with an extra button undone, more jewellery and Manolo Blahnik shoes. I wore it to work. To parties. On planes. I wore it for a meeting with Evelyn Lauder. I wore it to lunch with Jean-Paul Gaultier. I wore it in winter over a black poloneck and in summer over not much at all.

When it got older Shirty started to come on holiday with me, and we drifted around some very hot climates with our sleeves rolled up. In its very last months Shirty even started coming to the beach. But by then the rot had set in – literally. The silk had started to wear and tear. I had it mended several times to little effect, but even then I wasn't ready to say goodbye. Even after it accidentally got wet in the great laundry bag disaster of 98 and all the colours ran, I still kidded myself I was going to make Shirty into a fabulous cushion.

Of course I didn't, and now I have finally said goodbye to Shirty. And to my simple black sandals with buckles. The best shoes I have ever bought in terms of the style–comfort ratio. I've said goodbye to two little tops from Jigsaw that went under everything perfectly, and even to a couple of agnès b. faggoted cardigans, which I have finally decided I am fully over.

I did feel poignant for a moment as I finally threw them out – and I haven't given a thought to any of them since. But I'm not a millionaire yet, dammit.

Chain reaction

I am a liar. Many is the time I have exhorted women of a Certain Age to forgo cheap clothes in favour of owning fewer quality items that fit better and will last longer. This was rank hypocrisy. I adore cheap clothes. A trip to Pitt Street Mall or the Sportsgirl Centre to check out the latest 'offer' (retail jargon) at Portmans, Witchery and the like fills me with almost as much excitement as a stroll around Prada, Gucci or Chanel, where I know I will be treated more like a probable shoplifter than a potential shopper.

With the lack of really enormous smelly second-hand markets in Sydney and Melbourne (compared to, say, London or Paris, which are full of stinky piles of delicious dross), I think a foray through the racks of the chain stores satisfies the same atavistic foraging instinct that is sated by ransacking a flea market.

When I come out of Sportsgirl with a cute little evening bag for $25, or Portmans with a three-quarter sleeve V-neck T in fuchsia cotton for $30, I feel as if I have really scored. I've somehow got one over on the whole fashion conspiracy by finding something great in a cheap shop.

This is delusional. It's not an accident that Witchery has done a cotton cardie with frogging awfully similar to the agnès b. ones I keep going on about (actually, I am over them now, as previously mentioned) and Sportsgirl has done a good version of my favourite DKNY black jersey pants. These are not coincidences. The designers, buyers and trend scouts for our trendy chain stores know exactly what they are doing.

In fact, they are among the world's most frequent flyers, as it is part of their job description to jet around the globe looking at the newest shops and designer gear. Seriously. They window-shop for a living. Then they do 'interpretations' of the best bits they have seen and sell them to people like me at a fraction of the price of the real thing.

When they are not actually in New York, London and Paris checking out the new things by Callaghan, Narciso Rodriguez and YSL, they are going through copies of the latest Italian *Vogue* and US *Harper's Bazaar*, which they have airmailed to them the day they hit the newsstands in Milan and New York.

So it's hardly surprising that by the time chumps like me

get hold of the overseas mags and are instantly consumed with desire for a beaded dress, or a velvet coat like the ones Amber Valetta is wearing on page 143, they are already waiting for me, cut-price, in the mall. So who is the clever one, really? Them for knowing what the fashion victim is going to crave next, or me for getting it cheap?

Fashion buyers are always fiercely fashionably dressed themselves. These are the people who actually shop in Gucci and Prada. They wouldn't dream of wearing cheap clothes. They always buy This Season's Shoe and special 'pieces' by obscure designers.

When a piece of clothing is referred to as a 'piece', it means that it is made of an obscure (and usually scratchy) fabric and can't be worn without holding your stomach in. You usually need instructions on how to put it on and a fairly good knowledge of knots to keep it there. Designers who produce 'pieces' include Akira Isogawa, Comme des Garçons, Nicola Finetti and Issey Miyake.

Women who wear them always stand out at parties and look ever so slightly smug. They know they have spent their fashion dollars wisely on a few well-chosen 'pieces' that will always attract comment.

I wish I were the kind of woman who bought 'pieces', but I'm just not. I like stuff and lots of it. And that's the other great thing about cheap clothes. You can have so many more of them. Whatever age you are.

Fateful attraction

Clothing comes into our lives in many different ways. Sometimes we go out looking for it, money saved up, list of essentials written. This is when we find nothing that suits us. Then there are the outrageous shopping accidents which seem to happen when we can least afford them. Out we go for a new ironing-board cover (because we are so strapped for cash we have started taking in washing) and back we come with two cashmere cardigans and a delicately embroidered handbag. We feel so guilty we have to smuggle them past ourselves into the house.

Occasionally there are fashion purchases that transcend all the rules. They don't make you feel guilty and you certainly can't plan them. We don't look for them, they find us. Like love at first sight and the coincidences in romantic fiction, they are simply meant to be. This is synchronistic shopping. Karmic klothing.

Consider these examples:

(1) The Cesare Paciotti Shoes. Sometime ago, my boyfriend P. went to Melbourne to watch the Australian soccer team not get into the World Cup. While he was heartbroken about the two-all draw that bade the Socceroos toodle-oo, this tragedy paled compared with the incident with the blue suede shoes.

Brought up in southern Europe and very particular about his attire, P. had been scouring Sydney for something chic yet casual to wear sockless with his Calibre pants. They had to satisfy his very specific aesthetic – nothing clompy, nothing flashy, nothing cheap and nothing badly made. And that's what he found. Nothing.

But in Melbourne, where he says they really understand gentlemen's attire, he found them immediately. Supple blue suede loafers, like Tod's for men, he explained, with a really small silver snaffle.

Even the outrageous $500 price tag didn't disturb him. They were the right shoes and his clothing credo is you don't need to buy much if you buy the best. Oh, the disappointment when they didn't have his size. Oh, the number of times he told me about it.

So when we were back in Melbourne recently, there was much anticipation about going back to the shop because they might have new stock. They didn't. The shop didn't even exist any more.

Poor old P. was looking bravely at another summer in sandshoes, when his saintly patience with a clothing-fixated woman was rewarded. Agreeing to come into 'just one more' shop as I pursued my personal quest for a light-weight suit, there it was – a great pile of boxes of his perfect shoes. And not only did they have his size and his colour, they were on sale. $198. It was meant to be.

(2) The Green Velvet Suit. On a business trip to London, my friend Julie, a woman of great taste and a walking advertisement for investment dressing, was cruising Harvey Nichols in search of a simple black suit she could wear every week for the next ten years.

She found it (Claude Montana) and bought it, wincing at the price, but knowing it was a sensible buy. Moments later, she fell in love all over again – but with a much less suitable boy. A pale green velvet suit. She loved it, she looked gorgeous in it, she just couldn't justify it. But she thought about it all the way home on the plane, eventually ringing a girlfriend in London and persuading her to buy it, just so she would know it had gone to a good home.

Months later, strolling through David Jones's designer precinct, Julie saw her suit again. The right size, half the price. She wears it at least once a week. It was meant to be.

Women's wear daily

Not wearing black didn't work. Just wearing dresses didn't work. So in my ceaseless search for the ultimate clothing solution, I have been trying an experiment. Every day this week I have worn exactly the same outfit to the office: black pants and a black cashmere poloneck.

I don't think anyone has noticed.

I've noticed though. I've noticed that it only takes me five minutes to get dressed in the morning. I've noticed that I have felt effortlessly cosy, smart and comfortable every day. And I've noticed that I have had none of those terrible moments in the workplace lavs when you realise that, under fluorescent light, the outfit that looked pleasantly curve-hugging at home makes you look like a packet of cling-wrapped snags.

The reason no-one seems to have noticed my

unchanging aspect is partly because black pants and a poloneck is the kind of invisible commando's outfit you'd wear to rob the safe at the Hôtel de Crillon. But also, when you work with people every day, it actually becomes them you notice; the person and not their clothes. Blimey, there's a thought.

Mind you, I must have been noticing my colleagues' clothes a bit because I got the idea for my new work school uniform from them.

Of course, a lot of blokes wear the same suit to work every day; that's a given. In fact, it is one of the great professional advantages of being a corporate male. They've already slurped two lattes and read the *Fin Review* from cover to cover while you are still trying to find the right pair of opaques to go with that particular skirt. But some of the women at my work have uniforms, too.

Verna wears white every day. Always white pants, with various white jumpers, shirts and T-shirts. Her hair is white to match. I'd love to have a peek in her wardrobe – you'd need snow goggles. Suzy also wears daily pared-down ensembles with pants, but hers are in black and greys, with lovely chunky silver bangles to set it all off.

So those are their uniforms and mine is upmarket cat burglar, with slight variations each day: in the shoe department, because it's not good for the shoes or your feet to wear them two days in a row, and in the coat decision, because one day it was raining and another it was really freezing. The choice of coat led to a change of handbag, but this is minor compared with the usual frenzy of this-doesn't-go-with-that at 8.45 a.m.

During my first week in my winter plumage, I've had two business lunches, but they were with different people, so Wednesday didn't know what I wore on Tuesday (and I sponged the vongole sauce off the front so they wouldn't guess). And the night I had to go from work to a cocktail soiree, I just put on my good pearl earrings and smarter shoes.

So far, I don't think I smell. I gave the jumper a good sniff this morning and all I got back was a lungful of Calèche, so it seems that a quality natural fibre like cashmere just airs naturally each evening. And if you couldn't wear trousers for five days on the trot we'd all open dry-cleaning shops and retire after a year, although, once I get into the swing of it, I intend to do a weekly rotation with a similar pair of trews and wash the sweater on Sundays.

Hang on a minute – that sounds dangerously like a routine. Maybe this one-outfit wonder malarky isn't for me after all. Come to think of it, I did spend eleven years of my life creatively subverting a school uniform to express my individuality. Perhaps I'll just get up half-an-hour earlier instead.

News of the shoes

I have been in Paris for a week, staying in my natural habitat on the Left Bank – wedged in between the streets that women all over the world think of as Shoe Central. I haven't bought a single pair. I can't. There are too many nice ones.

Last time I was here, six months ago, I didn't buy any shoes because they were all too horrid, or stupid. Now I can't buy any because they are all too nice. The problem is, whichever pair I choose instantly means there is another pair I won't be able to buy. What if I realise later that I liked them better?

Of course, one option would be just to buy all of them (the Jackie Onassis manoeuvre), but for the sake of my financial future – and the weight of my luggage – I have given myself a budget of two pairs. But how can I pick just two from such a panoply of fabulous footwear? It's like the auditions for Scarlett O'Hara.

If I buy the fiercely pointy stiletto ankle boots I really want, I won't be able to buy the Prada mules in three shades of café au lait that I also really want. And if I buy those I won't be able to buy the cherry red rubber-soled, cute with a suit, rain-friendly walking shoes that I actually need.

Then there are the black patent court shoes in Yves Saint Laurent and the sand-coloured loafers in Gucci. Not forgetting the purple patent courts with a walkable heel from Sergio Rossi that my pal Naomi bought, Deeta's jewelled Maud Frizon mules, and the Jil Sander evening shoes that Melissa is obsessing about.

Because it's not just me. Every time I step out of my hotel I seem to bump into another fashion friend (we're all here for the shows) on her own Paris shoe mission. It's like a mantra. 'I'm just allowing myself two pairs . . . but I have to look at them all before I decide.'

Yesterday I bumped into Nicole on rue de Grenelle and recognised all too well the intensely focused expression in her eyes as she set off for rue du Cherche-Midi, almost audibly keeping an inventory of what she had already clocked in Michel Perry, Miu Miu, Christian Louboutin and Sergio Rossi. Then I ruined her life by telling her there were also some great things in Sacha.

'I'm just allowing myself two pairs,' she was saying, as she detoured down rue du Four.

Post script: This was written during the Paris ready to wear one October. For the record, I bought a pair of red graphic-print fabric Prada sling backs with wild red heels and the black pointy boots from Sacha. Both pairs have been on their maiden voyages – a preview of the re-make of *Shaft* and a frenzied night dancing with handsome young men at a Paris *boîte* respectively – and have been deemed a total success in terms of compliments received, relative comfort and 'lucky shoe' status.

Which just goes to show we were right all along – shoes bought in Paris really can change your life.

The untouchables

I have long lost track of how many fashion shows I've been to, but I still never fail to be amazed by how the eye can adjust to new looks.

Sometimes things look right immediately – like Prada's 1940s chiffon print dresses, with tweed coats and fur tippets. Other styles, like Fendi's spring/summer 2001 show, which was all mad World Wrestling Federation gold belts and shoulder pads Grace Jones would have baulked at in 1984, looked totally nuts at the time. But when I received the bound 'look book' from the company just a few weeks later, which has a snap of every outfit in it, I started planning my shopping list. Mmm, a ruched aubergine silk jumpsuit . . . tasty. I want pink fluoro cone-heeled pumps and I want them now.

But despite the human brain's amazing ability continually to tune into new ideas and aesthetics, there are some looks that should never see the catwalk. Yet they do. Every fashion season most of the following are witnessed, sometimes all in the one show:

- Hobble skirts. There is nothing more painful than seeing a model torturing her way down the catwalk in a stupid outfit she can't stride in. It looks dumb, takes too long, is reminiscent of foot binding and highly offensive to today's action babes. Plus I always feel so sorry for the poor model – it's like being at a play when someone forgets their lines or falls over. You lose the illusion. And want to go home.
- Anything with one leg. This never, ever works. When the loudest thing an outfit is saying is 'This is novel!' it's a guaranteed flop. One shoulder just scrapes through, but even one sleeve looks pretty dumb. And don't remind me of the one-cheeked bikini bottom I once witnessed.
- Nappy effects. Sometimes this is long and swingy, other times it is a snug Pamper – it's hard to say which is worse. Either way, male designers don't understand that fabric brought between the legs and fastened whispers 'Panty Pad' to most women and evokes ghastly memories of being thirteen. Gandhi was the last person who could pull off this look in public life.
- Hats and headdresses covering the entire face. Another

model torture. You can just see them thinking 'F * * *, f* * *, f* * *, I hate this!' as they totter along.

- Total body jewellery and other fashion contraptions. If you can't walk through a door without turning sideways, sit down, or raise a tea cup to your lips in it, I don't want to see it on a catwalk. I don't care about making a statement, it just gets in the way of seeing the actual gear.

- Bare breasts. Or breasts visible through sheer fabric. Great for getting coverage in the British gutter press, but really annoying as you have to narrow your eyes and imagine the same outfit with a nice neat slip underneath. Experience teaches that it will never look as good as Giselle's bouncing breasts, so it's a big cheat.

- Tailored jumpsuits on men, à la Torville and Dean. They make me prickle with embarrassment. It's something to do with the arrangement of the charcuterie counter, yet in the uncensored cut of a matador outfit this has quite another effect (phwoah!). Maybe it's just the incredible mimsy-ness of figure skating. And the terrible thought of anyone who does it ever having sex (yeeewww).

- Anything too redolent of a 'costume'. Whenever you see something that makes you hear an echo of Alfonso in the studio saying: 'I've got it!' (snaps fingers) 'Why don't we . . . ?' to a pack of simpering yes people, half his age,

129

who are all rolling their eyes behind his back and applying for other jobs on the sly, you know you're in for a cringe-a-thon. *The Wizard of Oz*, *Flamenco A Go Go* and *Show Boat* are three such experiences that come to mind.

Fashion senses

Like the other two best things in life – sex and food – clothes are sensual. They stimulate the senses. And to be any good, they have to delight all five of them. Okay, you probably stopped thinking the cuffs of your cardigan tasted delicious when you were around the age of ten months, but we do talk about well-dressed people having 'good taste' and we react to clothing in a very stomachy way. Clothes we don't like are pukey. They make us want to throw up. We don't say the bridesmaid dress she wanted us to wear was unattractive, we say it was *revolting*. It didn't make us want to weep, it made us want to *vomit*.

Sight is obviously involved. It's about a Look, so you want to enjoy looking at it. Touch is crucial, as you will know if you've ever worn a lambswool jumper next to the skin. Then a cashmere one. Or polyester pyjamas. Then silk ones. Or anything at all made of that frightful cack that pretends to be linen, but is actually made from scratchy palm trees.

You realise how important smell is whenever you encounter people who don't realise how important it is. These tend to be people who smoke. And people who retrieve garments from the washing basket for just one more little outing . . .

But in all this looking and smelling and feeling, I reckon sound is the sense it's easiest to forget. Unless you've ever worn creaky shoes in a library. That reminds you of it very quickly. You try peg-legging it, you try tippy-tiptoe, shuffling, goosestepping, hopping and still they creak. Step. Creak. Step. Creak. Step. Creak. Terrible.

Just last night I was walking up a dark street and I could hear this woman behind me in some kind of wooden clogs. Clonk, clonk, clonk. In the end I had to turn around to see what kind of cringing weirdo would wear such awful clonky shoes. She looked perfectly normal, she just sounded shocking – because she hadn't got off the carpet in the shoe shop. You must get off the carpet. You have to test drive shoes for sound as well as sight.

I recently walked away from buying a pair of shoes which I loved and adored, because when I walked around the shop in them fast they went slap-slap-slap against the soles of my feet and I suddenly understood where the term 'slapper' came from. By the same token, some men find the rat-tat-tat-tat of fast-moving stilettos on parquet extremely arousing. They know a taut calf and slender ankle are in the vicinity. Which is another reason to take sound into account in different clothing contexts. Instant erotica may be just the effect you want to achieve on a Saturday night, but at Monday morning's shareholders' AGM it's not such a bright idea. You might be correctly corporately attired from the ankle up, but if your shoes click-a-clack into the room like Gypsy Rose Lee, you've blown it. You might be thinking about the bottom line, but everyone else will be thinking about your bottom.

Men have to concern themselves in this regard with corduroy. The chafing sound of thighs rubbing together in corduroy trousers is extremely disturbing. It's a sort of squeaky, swishy noise. Sqweash sqweash sqweash. Here comes thunder thighs.

But not all clothing noises are bad. In fact, the great joy of wearing a full-bore evening number with a big swishy skirt is the swishy part. Rustling is great. Skirts always rustle in historical novels where bosoms heave and dashing men stride in with their spurs jangling. The tramp of heavy leather soles echoing down stone hallways can evoke terror or joy – is it Bluebeard in a murderous mood or Prince Charming in his handmade thigh-high riding boots?

Or just some twit who didn't test drive his slip-ons?

You beauty

We all know good-looking people, attractive people, pretty people and sexy people, but true beauty is something else entirely. I realised this the day I was sitting in a departure lounge at Paris airport and there was this woman I could not stop staring at. She just had something fascinating about her and I was desperately trying to figure out what it was. I kept trying to tear my eyes away because I know it's rude to stare, but I couldn't. She was mesmerising.

What was it about her?

She had interesting black clothes on, pretty blonde hair, a slim figure and terrific legs with really finely turned ankles. She had nice shoes on, too, but that wasn't it. There was more to it than that. Her face just seemed to have a glow about it. It was in permanent soft focus. She looked as if she were in her late forties, but her face was strangely ageless, childlike and wonderfully mature at the same time. And even though I was across the other side of the room, I could see the blue of her eyes clearly. Especially when she caught me staring at her and a look of pain seemed to flit across them.

That was when I realised it was Julie Christie.

Julie Christie is the most beautiful person I have ever seen. End of story. And I've interviewed just about every supermodel on the planet. She has an inner radiance that is like some kind of alien energy. Kate Moss and Claudia Schiffer and Elle Macpherson look beautiful in pictures, but I didn't find them overwhelming in real life. Gorgeous, but not too much to handle.

Naomi Campbell came close, as previously described, and Helena Christensen stood me still. My throat closed up when I had to interview her. I felt like a lumbering klutz, impossibly coarse, beside her. She is so beautiful she made me feel grubby. And, surprising as it may sound, Miss Kylie Minogue is much more astonishing in real life than she is in photos. She has a little bit of that alien fairy dust sprinkled on her, too. Maybe it's something to do with having a very large head-to-body ratio.

That may be one of the reasons why Bob Dylan is so charismatic in the flesh. He has a damn big head on him. Big heads must spark off some kind of primeval reaction in observers, because babies have them. Come to think of it, so do aliens. Anyway, I saw Mr Bob up close at a press conference in about 1986 and his presence filled the room in a way quite out of proportion even to his legendary status – and he sure ain't pretty no more. But you just couldn't take your eyes off him. I was totally smitten. It was like being at a press conference for Jesus.

The most truly beautiful man I have ever seen, however, was Imran Khan. He walked past me and my best friend, Josephine, at a cocktail party in London years ago and we just turned and looked at each other in amazement. The beauty of the face. The nobility of the bearing. The shoulderiness of the shoulders.

And I've never forgotten it because it prompted one of her better remarks. 'Well, he just bowled two maidens over . . .' she said.

The slippery slope

I've finally been skiing. Well, I didn't actually ski. I just went to see what everyone was wearing, because the main reason I've missed out on winter fun all these years is that I had too much outfit anxiety to go.

It wasn't that I was worried I would be hopeless on the piste. It goes without saying that I would be terrible at it, but after a lifetime of rivalling Mr Bean for negative sporting prowess I am used to physical humiliations of all kinds. What I really couldn't have endured is being incorrectly attired for the slopes – because when you are really bad at something, you have to do it in the right clothes.

If you're really good at something, it doesn't matter what you wear. I've got friends who have been skiing since they could stand and they swoosh down black runs in cocktail dresses and ballet tutus for a lark, but if you haven't got a clue you've got to have the gear. Not the ultimate, latest, most expensive professional rig-out – that looks really tragic on a beginner – but just right enough to fit in, so you look like you know what you're doing, but are having a bit of an off day.

It is also important, if you are a total klutz, that your kit on no account looks new, which was another reason for making an investigative expedition to the Snowy Mountains. A joyful afternoon's tobogganing gave me the chance to wear in my newly purchased Smurf hat and zip-front microfibre body warmer, so when I actually have my first ski lesson (some time next year), at least I won't be wearing that New Hat facial expression along with one of abject terror.

I bought those accent accessories in advance, but hired the rest of the outfit on the way to the snow, which was a hell of a risk. All the way to Cooma I was convinced that the only rental ski wear on offer would be white nylon with jade and jacaranda feature stripes – the kind of gear Sylvester Stallone's mother favours – so I was thrilled when I found some really acceptable black waterproof trousers and a Sportif bright red jacket I actually liked. It is, however, the last time I will be hiring footwear. Other people's feet. Enough said.

And there was another pleasant surprise about wearing padded clothing in public – one of the many aspects of skiing I had always regarded with horror – because why would anyone knowingly apply additional bulk to their frame? Would the Michelin Man wear a puffa jacket? Would Humpty Dumpty rug up in a doona coat? But in actual fact, rather than making me feel like the Pillsbury Doughwoman with a bad case of premenstrual water retention, my padded gear was very freeing. For once it was the clothes that were fat and not me. I could blame the whole thing on my pants.

It was worth going to Thredbo to spend a whole weekend without holding my stomach in.

Of course there were sleek snowrider babes strutting around in slinky black all-in-one ski suits and ski boots that made their pylon legs look even longer, but most people looked like me. Paddington Bear. Paddington Bear with a red nose and a lot to carry. But happy.

By Sunday afternoon, I was so relaxed in my ski gear I could hardly bear to take it off, even though it was about thirty degrees in the sun. Eventually, I was so emboldened that I found myself on a pair of skis, hurtling down the slope in a race, dodging trees and even doing the odd jump. The skis in question were attached to a $2 video game, but it was a start. And I had the right hat on while I was doing it.

Woolly thinking

You know, like, Einstein's theory of relativity and every-thing? Well, that space and time stuff is very interesting, but I think Tiny Einie missed out on a key area of application for it: shopping. So, as a tribute, I have been working on Alderson's Theory of Shopping Relativity.

It goes like this: the desirability of objects is relative to the other objects around them.

See? There is an ineluctable physical law that explains why you come back from holiday with a lot of terrible crap you never would have bought at home. It was the least horrible stuff among all the gruesome gee-gaws on offer – it is not until you see it in a broader context that you can acknowledge that it is repulsive. Just about every item of clothing ever bought in Bali falls into this category.

'Look at this dolphin-print 100 per cent viscose jump-suit – isn't it heaven?'

My theorem was conclusively proved during a trip to a very untouristy Greek island – so untouristy that it had nothing cute to buy. Even the postcards featured things like hydro-electric power stations. The most desirable item I could find was a jar of honey, and I couldn't wear that or get it through customs.

So imagine our excitement when we heard that the travelling gypsy market was making its annual visit to the neighbouring village that very week. What luck! I couldn't wait to snap up armfuls of colourful bangles, hand-embroidered peasant blouses and beautiful shawls.

Boy, was I in for a let-down. Just as gypsies have replaced colourfully painted wagons with nasty cara-vans, and darling piebald horses with ozone-zapping jalopies, they have replaced their exotic traditional attire with head-to-toe man-made fibres. This market was full of it.

You have never seen such a frightful array of ghastly tat. Hundreds of stalls winding along the narrow cobbled streets and nothing I wanted to buy. And believe me, I worked at it. First I went through it in great detail, convinced that, if I just kept looking, I would find the little old lady selling off her wedding trousseau. Then, when all hope faded, I went through it again just to marvel.

In the end I grew rather to love the piles of acrylic jumpers, the acres of Corfam shoes (similar to vinyl, but cheaper looking), the thickets of bristling nylon children's dresses and the racks of fake Nike sportswear.

But most interesting of all was observing my companions, who were still determined to find something to buy. They found it all right – natural wool vests and long johns as worn by shepherds. Natural wool in this context means it was practically baaaaaa-ing. The dags were still attached. It smelled so strongly of sheep that a border collie would have had you rounded up in a paddock in minutes.

Admittedly, the shape of the tops was quite nice – long sleeves and classic grandad's shirt necklines. But that's because they were Grandad's shirts. They smelled like Grandad had just taken them off. Or died in them. I have rarely seen more unpleasant objects, but my companions carried on like they had just discovered pashminas. There was wild talk of exporting in bulk and they couldn't believe I wasn't snapping up a few to wow everyone at Fashion Week.

At dinner that night they all wore them, wittily worked back with bandannas and T-shirts. But guess what? I haven't seen those items since. I think when they were unpacked at home, their owners probably sprang back in alarm and called the exterminators.

Because that is the second rule of Alderson's theory of shopping relativity. The whole is greater than the sum of the parts – and what you have when you get home is just one of the parts.

A friend like Ben

Thank you for asking me, but I'm afraid I won't be able to come out for the next few weeks. I'm rather busy, as a little white stranger was delivered this morning. It is five years since I have heard the patter of a tiny spin cycle in my own home and I'm staying in to bond with Ben.

Ben Dix the washing machine, that is. He is my new pride and joy, and I won't be happy until every garment, towel, sheet and tablecloth I own has passed through his porthole door and come out clean and fresh and smelling of the free fabric conditioner he brought with him.

When my parents first got an automatic washing machine, in about 1970, they pulled up chairs to watch it go round, washing and rinsing and spinning all by itself. They thought it was miraculous – no more mangle! I thought they were nuts, but now I'm trying to figure out how I can get the sofa into the bathroom so I can watch Ben perform the cold wash in comfort. And I can't wait for that climactic moment when he switches from spinning to drying.

Because Ben is a combined unit. He can wash and dry all on his own. That's why he cost the price of a one-bedroom unit in Perth.

Apart from his technical wizardry (he heats up his own water and judges the minimum amount he can use for each load completely unaided, because he cares deeply about the environment), Ben represents a return to adulthood for me, after half a decade living in units that simply could not accommodate any whitegoods beyond a fridge and a toaster.

For that time my Saturdays were a trudge of humungous bags in and out of lifts to communal laundries, only to find all the machines were already full. Or having got up at 7 a.m. to secure one, of going back an hour later to find my pile of precious clothes suppurating on top of the drier while someone else's gear purred smugly inside.

In one building where we had a rooftop washing line, I came back to check on my non-fast coloureds load to find a woman moving my damp whites out of the sunshine into a dank corner in favour of her own, because hers were 'wetter'. I went back later and threw a pair of her knickers off the roof.

After that I stopped hanging my stuff out to dry for fear of reprisals, so it was a choice of festooning it around the flat, like the rags at the site of a recent vision of the Virgin Mary, or nuking it in the communal driers.

They certainly do the job (you could fire pots in them) but the process involves first taking the pubic lint out of the drier after someone else's turn, which makes me feel sick. Irrational I know, because it is all freshly washed (otherwise it wouldn't be in the drier, would it?), but I don't want to touch other people's sock fluff and under-scunder plunder at any stage of the wash cycle.

Mind you, at least the apartment buildings here have laundries. In London you have to go to a public laundrette. The horror, the horror. The last time I ever used one I saw a man inspect a pair of trousers he was about to wash, then take off the ones he was wearing and put them in a machine instead. And believe me, he looked nothing like the bronzed love god in the Levi's commercial.

Barbie's my kind of girl

Somebody gave me a 'Barbie Through the Decades' calendar for Christmas. And, let me tell you, I was as excited by that telltale pink tissue paper wrapping as I would have been by the blue of a Tiffany box or the orange of a Hermès carrier bag. So far I haven't even broached the cellophane wrapping (too special), but just by looking at the small photos on the back, I can tell you that in the 1988 shot Barbie is dressed by Ferré (she has wide-belted leather pants tucked into boots and a floor-length coat; she's walking the dogs), and 1989 could be Valentino (it looks like something Joan Collins would wear to Ascot) or Lacroix (colour, sweetie, colour).

For the 1997 pic, she has raided my wardrobe. This picture has four Barbies dressed in my clothes. Black jersey pants and T-shirts, black turtlenecks and tight skirts, with black opaque tights and feature handbags (one is a camel-coloured leather hand-held, just like mine). The only things I'm not very keen on are the belts, but then Barbie has always over-accessorised.

But really it's not surprising that Barbs and I should be dressing alike. We've been friends for an awfully long time. We're practically the same age for one thing (well, she is a little bit older actually, if you have a good watch) and we share all the same interests. We even have the same favourite colour (pink).

I can't remember when I got my first Barbie, but I have adored her ever since. I had a whole commune of them living in an old hatbox, plus a couple of less glamorous Pommie chicks called Sindy, a Patch with one leg longer than the other who was a real waste of pocket money (no high heels), and a weird Ken with moulded hair. He was a total wimp.

My preferred Barbie boyfriend was my brother's Action Man because he had a much better body and wore uniforms. Plus he had a scar on his face which I thought was dreamy. Barbie liked it when he took his clothes off and one day I pulled off one of his legs in my eagerness to remove a boot. That took a bit of explaining, but my brother thought it was quite good for realistic battle scenes.

My Barbies had a pink-and-white plastic wardrobe complete with curly hangers, a dining table and sideboard with all requisite cutlery, china and candelabra, a second-hand horse, an outfit for every occasion, a white Scotty dog and a black poodle. I made a whole apartment for her (based on Mary Tyler Moore's – I had never seen an apartment in 1967) under my dressing-table, where extremely complex sitcoms and romantic encounters took place (one of them leading to that severed limb). It was a whole world under there.

I think Barbie was good for me. Of course I know all the feminist arguments against gender stereotyping and her ridiculously unattainable Hugh Hefner fantasy physique. But while I'm not sure which way she is less correct – anatomically or politically – I still think she helped to shape me in a positive way.

Sure, I spent hours mixing and matching her outfits and doing her hair, but I also spun great imaginative fantasies about her life in that apartment with Ken, Action Man and all her girlfriends. My Barbie had a pretty good life. Not that different from the one I lead today actually (especially if Ken turned out to be gay). I never felt I was supposed to look like her, just as I never expected to be rescued from a tower by a prince on a white horse or to meet a mouse who talked in a high-pitched voice. Barbie is a fantasy. And if she gives children an interest in co-ordinating their clothes, she's all right by me.

Just don't take her advice on accessories.

Doggie style

I don't want to wear clothes any more. I'm sick of them. I want fur. Not a fur coat, yucky yucky, but my own fur. Attached. And a tail. I can't think of anything more stylish than having a tail. You could wag it if you were pleased to see someone – wouldn't that be nice? And I've always thought I would like to be able to express my displeasure by snatching my tail out last as I left a room, in an animal version of giving the finger. The lady cats in 'Tom and Jerry' used to do things like that, and sometimes they would make their tails into beckoning fingers around doorways, which always got Tom hot and bothered.

I once asked the late fashion designer Franco Moschino if he would make me a jacket with a remote-control tail. I suggested the handset could be concealed in a pocket, so

I could swish it like a cat when impatient, thump it like a dog when excited and perform the exit described previously when in a snit. I also suggested I could curl it over my arm at cocktail parties. He thought it was a top idea and I think he might have made it for me if he hadn't been so cruelly taken from us.

A remote-control tail would be something, but I think I would just actually like to be a dog. They are so marvellous. Dogs are some of the most chic people I know. Lucy, who lives in the fashionable Gotham City building in Elizabeth Bay, Sydney, knows everybody. She is greeted wherever she goes. And if she likes you, you get her special toothy smile. She loves parties and always puts on her pearls when people are coming over. She walks differently when she's wearing them.

Suzy rides around Woollahra in her own stroller. She's a little bad-tempered (she has a sign warning she might bite you), but she has quite a regal air in her chariot. Horace, who also lives in Woollahra, clearly has aristocratic blood, too. The chihuahua side of the family has given him the most finely boned legs since Princess Di. His barrel body comes from the Jack Russell side, which no-one likes to mention.

Miss Emerald, a poodle of the 'hood, sits outside all the shops and waits patiently. She has such decorum. Perhaps she is hoping Freddie will walk by. Freddie is a golden retriever so handsome he could star in Ralph Lauren advertisements. He is the male supermodel of the dog world. He looks like a rower.

Flea lives nearby, too. She's rather reclusive in her old age and fond of lying on the bed all day in her furry negligee. But put on a disco hit and she's straight onto the dance floor.

Those are the local dogs. Out bush is Zambia, a large black standard poodle, but very feminine. She sleeps in an old Mary Poppins pram. You couldn't expect her to sleep on the ground with her son Juica. He's more of your stubbies-and-Blundstones type. He'd be happy sleeping in the back of a panel van.

Overseas there is Scarpia, an opera-loving pug with his own Hermès collar. He can't wait for the annual Pug Picnic, where all the pugs meet up so their humans can play together. Scarpia thinks they all look so sweet. You'd almost think they were dogs, the way they carry on.

But so far, for canine style there has been no-one to match the mighty Olympia, a black labrador of great refinement. A party girl like Lucy, she used to wear a tutu to her soirees.

Olympia is no longer with us. She was claimed in London by a council truck, but I often think of her glossy head and the weekend we spent together in Wales, where we all played dress-ups. Olympia wasn't sure how good she looked in the headscarf, but was prepared to wear it for the photo. Now I like to think of her up in heaven, happily gnawing on one of Franco Moschino's shoes.

Cheap tricks

Beware hidden charges. Clothing convenience can go down as well as up. Just as you would minutely scrutinise a mortgage or insurance policy, always read the small print on any garment you are considering buying. And I don't just mean the actual small print on the laundry label (although, of course, you may want to rethink the purchase of a white shirt that has Dry Clean Only status), but also the metaphorical small print, in terms of the hidden cost of your new purchase. They can really sneak up on you.

While the prospect of a lifetime of dry cleaning (it's the pain of it, as much as the price, isn't it?) is an obvious deterrent to buying a white cashmere trouser suit, it can also catch you out on something as reliable looking as a pair of black pants. If they have stretch in the fabric they can go baggy at the knees after two wears, requiring dry cleaning to snap them back into shape. In the same group there are skirts that get impossibly creased after one wear, and beaded tops that require special service hand cleaning.

Then there are alterations and maintenance to consider. My favourite vintage (read stinky op-shop) fake fur jacket was such a bargain: just $30 for something that looks like it came straight out of Fendi's last show (except only nylons died for it). Little did I realise that the initial $30 was barely more than a deposit.

The first hidden cost was the NASA dry cleaning required to get the terrible stench out of it. To remove the frightful pong (eau de damp bedsit), it had to go into a special ozone chamber which cost three times as much as normal cleaning.

It smelled much better when it came out, but the lining hung in shreds where the ozone had eaten it, so I had to buy new lining fabric and pay a tailor to put it in. Then I decided the cheap plastic buttons needed to be replaced to do justice to the splendid bishop purple silk lining. And if time is money, I spent plenty finding the perfect woven leather fast-eners to set off the sheen of the luxuriant fake fur. When I had finished fooling around with it, that $30 jacket would have cost me nearly five times as much. Fortunately, I adore it, but I would have thought much harder about splashing out on a novelty fun fur car coat if I had known it was going to turn into a $150 novelty fun fur car coat.

Speaking of cars, this aspect of fashion shopping is very similar to the experience of buying a new car. You get all excited about the price – 'Look, darling, it's only $18 000 drive-away!' – and rush off to the showroom. Then, after swaggering around a bit because you're not just looking, you are actually going to buy a car, you sit down with someone young enough to date your best friend's children to discuss terms and go through the choice of 'extras'.

The car comes, of course, with the standard cardboard wheels, he tells you, sitting up straight in his high chair. But for just $3 000 more, you can have metal wheels. For an additional $10 000, you can have the ones in the picture of the car that brought you here.

The last time I bought a new car (okay, the only time), I felt triumphant when I screwed the saleschild down on the mats.

I got my mats for nothing. Boy, was I gloating when I left that showroom, until I realised he had sold me a set of black numberplates for an additional $100. Every time I see one of Mickey's cousins (sorry, that's the tragic name I use for all cars the same colour and model as mine) with perfectly functional regular numberplates, I hang my head in shame.

That $100 would have paid for the renovations on my car coat.

Dirty looks

In early adolescence, my brother Nick developed an unhealthy obsession with bikies. It was inspired by an unpleasant little paperback called *Hell's Angel*, which he read with great fascination. My mother said she was just glad to see him reading.

As a prissy nine-year-old swotty squit, I was appalled by the book (which I read as soon as I could lay my fat little hands on it) and the magazines that followed it into the house. They were called something like *Hog* and featured a loathsome cartoon character called Spider, and Spider's Ol' Lady, who was his girlfriend.

Horrid things happened to Spider's Ol' Lady, which were meant to be hilarious but which I always found very upsetting – but it didn't stop me making secret forays into Nick's bedroom to read the latest issue when it arrived.

Hog also featured pages of photos of recent bikie social gatherings, which included lots of real-life 'ol' ladies' sitting on the back of chopped hogs (motorbikes) wearing leather shorts and no tops and smiling at the camera over a can of beer. They all wore rings on their forefingers, I noted. I found them fascinating, like the bike equivalent of *Tatler's* social pages.

But the worst aspect of Nick's bike period – even worse than when he 'chopped' my bicycle for me, adding ape hanger handlebars and removing girlie extras like mudguards and ting-a-ling bells – was his 'Originals'.

'Originals' are jeans and denim jackets that bikies get when they first become bikies. Part of the initiation into the 'chapter' (according to *Hell's Angel*) is for all the other bikies to stand in a lovely fairy ring and urinate on them. You never ever wash your Originals.

The stinkier the better. And you have to wear them every day.

Nick's Originals comprised a saggy denim jacket from which he removed the sleeves and then lined the armholes with pieces of rabbit fur taken off his ex-army parka. Buttons were wrenched out and replaced with crude thongs. His 'chapter' details were stencilled on the back in felt pen.

I don't quite think he went through the full initiation ritual, but by the time a thirteen-year-old boy has worn an outfit every day for several months (putting it on straight after school each night and cycling at great speed on his 'chopped hog'), it does acquire a certain hum. He never allowed his bikie gear to get washed and, not wishing to quash creative outpouring of any kind, our mother left him to it.

I was outraged by every aspect of Nick's Originals. I had to look at them across the table every teatime and I had to sit next to them on car journeys. But what made me really furious was that he was allowed to wear his Originals to the Rum Hole on my birthday. (The Rum Hole was the nearest proper restaurant to our beach house in Wales and, with prawn cocktail in little aluminium cups, steak Diane, black forest gateau and plenty of doilies, it was the acme of sophistication to me. How could we be seen there with Nick in his Originals?)

I can remember speaking to my mother in outraged indignation about it: 'You're not going to let Nick wear his Originals to the Rum Hole are you?' But it didn't have any effect. Nick and his Originals were not to be parted until girls became more interesting to him than motorbikes.

So I can't remember what I wore to my tenth birthday dinner, but I clearly recall shaggy-haired Nick in his Originals, with a shrunken brown T-shirt and horrid jeans that hung around his hips. I insisted on walking in separately.

All of which is a long way of telling you that I won't be embracing the 'dirty denim' trend which is upon us. I don't care if Chanel do make them. They all look like Nick's Originals to me.

Ms Alderson regrets

Nine outfits I wish I had never worn (or: Why didn't I listen to my mother?).

1   A buttercup-yellow skivvy. A tomato-red Laura
    Ashley smock pinafore. Yellow bell bottoms.
    Red-and-yellow 10-centimetre platform clogs
    with anchor motif. Yellow-and-red stripy socks. I am
    not making this up. I wish I was. 1973.
2   A plastic carrier bag worn as a boob tube. It was a
    great look. Until someone in the mosh pit (not that
    we called them that then – they were more like
    pogo pits) decided to tear it off. I managed to
    salvage enough of it to stay to the end of Johnny
    Thunders and the Heartbreakers' set, but I wasn't
    jumping up and down, let me tell you. Or was it

the Boomtown Rats? 1977.

3   Original land girl corduroy jodhpurs. Leather riding
    boots to the knee. A boy's tweed sports jacket.
    A viyella shirt. A yellow V-neck jumper. A cravat
    with a fox motif. A yellow silk pocket handkerchief.
    A tweed shooting cap. It was my first day at a
    secretarial college for young ladies in Wolverhampton
    and I wanted to make an impression. I did. Nobody
    talked to me. 1977.

4   A fuchsia-pink spandex tube skirt (homemade).
    A nylon fuchsia leotard. Fuchsia-pink stiletto mules
    with marabou pompoms. Fuchsia blusher as eye-
    shadow. Permed hair. Actually, I don't regret that
    one. It was fabulous. 1977.

5   Old Levi's with rips in the knees. A not-very-nice
    motorcycle jacket in leather as stiff as cardboard
    which I had liberated from my boyfriend. A stripy
    Breton fisherman's jumper. Bleached hair with
    roots growing back. I did not look like Bananarama.
    I looked like Spider's Ol' Lady and the local chapter
    of 'greasers' (bikers lite) was awfully pleased to see
    me. I was awfully pleased to see my bus coming.
    1980.

6   Old men's brown cord trousers held up with a
    Scout belt – and red clip-on braces. A collarless
    shirt. A red bandanna. Sensible lace-ups. I was

young and lissom, what was I doing? Trying to look like Benny Hill in country bumpkin mode? I didn't even like Dexy's Midnight Runners. 1981.

7 A cheap black polyester lace corset. Some black-and-white plaid polyester taffeta ruched into a homemade interpretation of Lacroix's puffball skirt. Hair with a bright pink rinse through it. Cheap diamanté jewels. Nylon opera gloves. I don't dare to remember what the shoes were. It was a gorgeous Scottish ball and I was surprised that the fresh-faced boys in their dashing kilts would rather dance with the equally fresh-faced girls in their floral Laura Ashley ball dresses than me. Thank heavens for darling James, who would rather have danced with the fresh-faced boys himself but reeled me expertly around the floor all night. 1981.

8 A fluorescent lime-green thick-knit acrylic jumper. It was one of those high-fashion trends that could be knocked off instantly by the chain stores and I was sucked right in. What a vile object. The only up side of the experience was that I wasn't taken in by the lime and orange debacle of a few summers ago. 1983.

9 My friend E. Jane Dickson's black jersey dress, with the skirt pinned up into a bizarre Austrian-blind effect with hidden safety pins, because she is

180 centimetres and I am 157 centimetres. It was my first big black-tie fragrance launch. I had no idea what to wear. I must have looked insane, but I had an awfully nice time. There was champagne and everything. 1985.

Throwaway lines

How do we feel about disposable clothes? A very space-age notion, isn't it? It's what we all expected to be wearing in the year 2000. Zip-up jumpsuits made from paper fibres that heat up and cool down automatically according to climatic conditions. One size adjusting to fit all. Colour changes according to thought patterns (pink = 'You're sweet'; green = 'Not so close, death-breath'). Built-in video-phone wristwatches. A little velcro pocket for your lunch capsules and integral straps to attach you to your solar-powered Toyota flight pack. Throw it away every night and get another from the pod's supply in the morning.

We never thought we would still be catching the bus in dresses and raincoats, did we? Or hand washing cashmere jumpers and best undies on Sunday nights, just like our mothers and their mothers before them? But while women's clothes are fundamentally the same as they have been for eighty years (more than 100 years for men), there are signs that disposable fashion is upon us.

Not disposable fashion in the sense that the It shoe of the season will, without fail, become the Twit shoe of next season, but clothes that are bought in the full knowledge that they will only be good for one or two wears before they hit the charity bin or the duster drawer.

This phenomenon first arose with the crisp white T-shirt, as worn under the crisp Helmut Lang pants-suit by Smart Corporate Babes (of both sexes). The problem was that after a few washes, the crisp white T became the dingy whitish T and the SCBs started buying their favourite Petit Bateau, Gap, Country Road, Bonds etc. variations in bulk – and ditching them like used tissues as soon as the drabs set in.

This led quickly to the princessy end of the SCB set becoming so addicted to the snap of a new T-shirt, with its smooth, crisp fabric dressing – as beguiling as the smell of a new car – that they could only bear to wear each T-shirt once before giving it the heave-ho.

Maybe it's my sensible Scottish blood rising to the surface (ne'er waste an oat if ye want ye groats, and that kind of thing), but I find that concept deeply immoral. The sheer shameless waste is repugnant in itself. Then there are the ruinous implications for the environment, as cotton is one of the most pest-bedevilled of crops, requiring lavish spraying and squirting of noxious chemicals to reach profitable maturity.

And the box-fresh T-shirts are just the start of the disposable trend. Swedish chain Hennes & Moritz was an absolute smash hit when it opened in New York recently. Its philosophy? Style over quality, forget service and sell it cheap. And I mean CHEAP. A report in *New York* magazine described febrile fashionistas queuing up to get into the thronged shop to snap up 'throwaway' one-season-wonder fashion items such as zebra-print halter-tops for US$6 each. One girl was buying ten $6 white bikinis – one for each Hamptons weekend.

Even apart from the craven waste, this throwaway attitude takes the heart and soul out of dressing. How cold and calculating you must have to be to discard a garment after just one outing. I like to build a relationship with my clothes. Over the years they can become like pets: part of the family, with fond memories – and a bit smelly around the extremities.

It's also a very expensive way to dress. Consider this: if you buy one ultra-fine cashmere T-shirt, it will air out every night, need washing only once a week and come out looking like new every time. And while it will cost a terrifying $450 up front, after just nineteen outings the cost per wear comes down to less than one environment-wrecking, one-wear $25 cotton rag ($23.68 to be precise).

As my partner says, with European smugness, whenever he sees me retrieving yet another amoeba-shaped chain-store T-shirt from the washer – I'm not rich enough to buy cheap clothes.

Fashion survivor

I've had this great idea for a TV show. It's called 'Survivor'. Oh, apparently someone else has already used that name. Okay then – I'll call it 'Fashion Survivor'.

This is what happens: we take sixteen fashionistas and fly them into a city they have never visited before – but their luggage never arrives! All they have left are the clothes they're wearing, their hand baggage and $500 credit left on their charge cards. Scary!

We watch as they battle against the elements to dress themselves without any of their favourite pieces. We hold our breath as they struggle to put together a new mini wardrobe, shopping in unfamiliar territory among brands they don't know, with a budget they'd normally spend on one pair of designer sunglasses – testing stuff!

The real fun starts as we see them scrambling to meet

the daily challenges. Scraping up a look for an industry cocktail party, an important work lunch and a smart-casual Easter weekend, without any of their favourite shoes, scarves or feature bags. This is life on the edge!

Adding to the tension – every three days one fash-ionista will be voted 'out' by the rest of the style tribe and deliberately not be invited to an In Crowd boutique opening.

It's cruel and ruthless – we will see him or her in tears as they ring the PR to see if their invite has been 'lost in the post' – but that's life out there in the fashion jungle. Brutal and savage. Only the innately chic will survive.

Outwit. Outplay. Outlast. Out of style.

This reality television proposal was inspired by my own experiences of sending a suitcase via 'unaccompanied bag-gage' from Heathrow airport.

'That second suitcase takes you over the luggage weight limit and will cost you an extra $900,' said the infant on the desk at Virgin Airlines.

'We will deliver to your door within seven days!' said the poster at the unaccompanied baggage desk.

'Where do I sign?' said I.

After three weeks I was still waiting for that suitcase to arrive. The 'seven day' shippers told me it was held up by foot and mouth disease and Easter. What did I care why? I just wanted it back – it contained all my best clothes.

My Helmut Lang day suit. My Helmut Lang T-shirt. My Lawrence Steele pencil skirt. My Martin Margiela boat neck. My agnès b. stripy matelot top. My best dark red leather coat. And much more I'd forgotten about, having been separated from it for so long.

I can't begin to describe how dislocated I felt without it all. I kept going to my wardrobe, like a mother bird returning to a nest that has been destroyed by a predator, only to remember, as I started to rake through the empty hangers, that my babies weren't there.

My clothing children were sitting in a warehouse some-where – I didn't even know in what country – possibly in a bath of anti-foot-and-mouth disinfectant. I didn't know when – or if – I would ever see them again.

This situation forced me to become extremely creative with regard to the wardrobe remnants I had left. Garments which hadn't seen daylight for half a decade were being brought out for an airing. 'Mistake' purchases were finally proving that I wasn't completely insane when I bought them. Items that had been lost in the dark recesses of cup-boards for seasons were making comebacks not seen since Barry White was re-discovered by Groove Armada.

In some ways it was good to be stretched to the limits of my sartorial survival endurance, but I was getting close to reaching breaking point. One morning I realised I was going to have to break one of my tightly held personal ethic codes and wear black to the races on a Saturday. And that was bad enough to make me vote myself off the show.

Down and dirty

Last October I saw a rock star in the Hôtel de Crillon in Paris. He must have been a rock star because no ordinary citizen would have been allowed in the doors of that august institution looking as bad as he did. And he wasn't just walking through the lobby for the hell of it – he emerged from the guest lift, so he was clearly staying there.

The little group I was having a drink with had got all dressed up for our night out on planet posh. I was so excited I'd had my hair done and put on my best new kinky boots. But the mystery rock star was wearing a mad old brown tweed coat that was much too big for him and looked as though it was tied at the waist with string (it wasn't, but it could have been).

His trousers were way too long and flapping around his scuffed hobnail boots and, looking at his hair, you would have thought he had been sleeping recently in a hedge, rather than one of the world's most elegant hotels. He was also savagely unshaven – which could have been the name of his band, for all I know.

If he'd shuffled out of there and taken up residence nearby with the poor old grimy clochards who sleep under the bridges of the Seine, no-one would have given him a second look, but in that setting we were obsessed with figuring out who he was, especially as he had that Please Don't Look At Me famous person's expression on his face. (I don't think it was Eddie Vedder from Pearl Jam, but he did look very Seattle.)

Celebrity identity aside, what really fascinated me about mystery manky man was the effort it must have taken to look so scruffy. The only way you could give a coat that found-in-an-ancient-peat-bog effect, without actually stealing it from a real tramp, would be to throw it on the floor after every wearing and jump up and down on it a lot. It would also help to roll around in puddles and then leave it bundled up wet in the boot of a car. Or you could put it in the basket of a very old and incontinent dog.

The same studied anti-grooming can also be observed in backpackers. They delight me with their aggressively unwashed posturing. I can watch them for hours, twisting their hair into ever more impenetrable tangles and scuffing along in ancient sandals.

It makes me feel like Jane Goodall observing chimps. The older, more mismatched and droopy their clothes, the happier they seem to be. They even sit scruffily, all hunched down, or with their feet up on the seat in front, or cross-legged. Whether they are in a café, a cinema, or on a bus, the point is to make it obvious that they would much rather sit on the ground – or, even better, a nice filthy gutter – than on anything as bourgeois as a seat. They're hilarious.

Of course, the reason there is such prestige in looking as scruffy as possible in that particular and peculiar microcosm of Western society, is that it's one of the things that marks you out as being a cool 'traveller' as opposed to a loathed 'tourist'. This is a very important distinction for middle-class kids on the well-trod gap-year trail.

The lark of it is that they think they'll mingle more closely with Third World locals by wearing the same T-shirt and scuffs for several months, accessorised with a few crappy bangles and thread bracelets, when the native population would be thrilled to have the chance to wear a nice smart suit – or Lil' Kim's head-to-toe Dior – if only they could.

And that's what I find so fascinating about the contrived grunge meisters. Whether they're bona fide rock stars, or English public school boys slumming it in

Australasia before Oxford, it's the ones who have been born with a choice who affect to look like down-and-outs. Which makes it the diametric opposite of ghetto fabulous. Aren't we humans funny?

Seeing stars

I saw Cameron Diaz on King Street this afternoon. I saw Jennifer Lopez at the taxi rank, Pamela Anderson in the bank and Jennifer Aniston on the escalators in DJ's. I spotted Sarah Jessica Parker in a restaurant last night and Fran Drescher has worked in my local newsagency for ages. Well, I didn't really see them, I saw their clones and, if you go out and look, you'll be able to see them, too.

Over the past couple of years, fashion has become obsessively focused on celebrities. Rather than following designer trends, style-conscious gals now seem to dress like their favourite famous person – and whatever designer trends she is following.

Once you get your eye in, you can see it so clearly, and it's quite a good game, if you're waiting at the bus stop, to spot who is strolling by. If you have a like-minded friend with you, you can add a competitive element to it (and it would be unAustralian not to) by scoring points for who spots them first:

JENNIFER LOPEZ – FIVE POINTS. You can always pick 'J-Lo', as His Royal Puffiness insisted she be called, by the large expanses of tanned and oiled skin on display. The clothes – usually a dress, usually jersey – will be skimpy, the overall vibe sultry. There's a lot of toned calf action in high-heeled mules, looking up through dark eyes and, of course, maximum booty. Lips are pouty and eyeliner mandatory.

JENNIFER ANISTON PITT – THREE POINTS. It's the sleek blow-dry, it's the slick lip gloss, it's the slinky jersey separates and it's the sick-making abs. At weekends, it's the slouchy cargo crops and the singlet. At all times, it is all about shoulders and collarbones, chunking in the highlights, swishy hair and mascara, mascara, mascara. A low score because there are so damn many of them.

SARAH JESSICA PARKER – SIX POINTS. A higher score because you don't see much curly blonde hair in our city centres, where the blow dry rules. The score goes down a point with every 5 kilometres you travel in any direction out of town, where mousse and scrunch drying remain more popular. The rest of the outfit is all about shoulders and heels. Strapless, backless, etc., but with less dependence on jersey than other celeb clones. There's a raw silk thing going on here. Interesting chokers. Bangles.

LINDA EVANS – SEVEN POINTS. A high score for this look because of the increasing rarity value. Time was when the ash blonde fringe with back-combed crown, and refrigerator shoulders in electric blue silk could be seen on every city street. Now a Linda spotting is something to celebrate. With the 1980s fashion revival upon us, the cone heels and golden jewellery will return, but I don't reckon we'll see that hair – or clip-on earrings – again on anyone except a Linda clone.

FRAN DRESCHER – EIGHT POINTS. Like Sarah Jessica, you will find a greater concentration of Frans outside your CBD inner ring, but wherever you find her, enjoy and celebrate. Isn't it wonderful that someone is prepared to invest that much money on hair and nail products? And so much time in maintaining her own very particular standards of grooming?

CAMERON DIAZ – TEN POINTS. This is the double somersault with pike and twist of the celeb clone-spotting finals. Why? Because Cameron is the über chick, the goddess, the best pal we all wish we had. Occasionally you see her, all long legs in dark denim, feathery blonde bob and singlet, eating a hot dog and looking like she's just heard a really good dirty joke.

One final rule of the game: scores gained by looking in the mirror do not count.

Tying one on

The esteemed former editor of British *Vogue*, Beatrix Miller, once said that she could always tell if a prospective employee was a '*Vogue* girl' by the way she tied her scarf. Right scarf, you got the job (and prayed you had a large enough private income to support yourself while you did it). Wrong scarf, forget it.

I often reflect on the scarf test when I am tying one on (a scarf, not a wild night in a line-dancing bar) and wonder if my knot and flourish would have passed the Miller Test. I'm awfully fond of scarves of all kinds and do have a few variations in the knotting and arranging departments, if I say so myself.

My current favourite is the simple Swallows and Amazons reef knot (over, round, up, through, under, round, through) resulting in two rabbit-ear ends and a smooth knot, mid-thorax, preferably showing off a nice bit of pattern. This is a jaunty look for smaller and softer scarves. (Please note: the scarf is rolled before tying, rather than arranged in a neat point at the back, unless you actually want to look like a Mountie.)

Another favourite is the Pseudoblouse – a large, sleek, silk scarf simply folded over at the chest and tucked into the waistband of pants, with no knot. This is excellent when you want to wear nothing, or just a scraggy old T-shirt, under a jacket and it shows off beautiful designs better than most.

The Lady Cravat – when you go over, all the way round again, up and through, but don't tuck it back through the knot as you would with a tie – is great for a formal look and when you want to keep your neck warm. It's a secure knot that won't let the scarf gradually slip off when you're not looking, which is a problem with the amateurish-looking once-over knot.

On occasion, I have even been known to tie a small scarf around my wrist, or a medium-sized one around my ponytail. Get me. I feel very *on* with Beatrix Miller in both these looks, but I have to admit it – I stole them. The wrist action from a lady in a dress shop in Paris and the ponytail manoeuvre from my friend Pippa, a fashion stylist. She's a Melbourne gal who once worked for Aussie *Vogue* and is now a resident in London. Beatrix Miller would have loved her. Why? She just has that indefinable quality that

Ms Miller could read in a scarf.

I was prompted to ponder all this scarfery on Bandanna Day, when the charity CanTeen, which gives support to young people living with cancer, sells bandannas to raise funds (bandannas because chemo- and radiotherapies make your hair fall out and it gets a bit draughty, as I know all too well).

They were selling them in the kiosk at work and, as I looked around the office, many of my workmates had the brightly coloured pieces of fabric strapped onto their person. There were some rolled and tied around foreheads like Dennis Hopper in *Easy Rider*, there was the odd Latino skullcap and a couple of Gidgets. There were deliberately cheeky multiple bandannas hanging from various jeans pockets (go Timmo), one tied around the head like an Alice band and held on with hair slides (you can't be too careful) and one that seemed just to have landed randomly on the head, like a cat from a high window.

How did I wear my bandanna? It was on my head, my wrist, my neck and my ponytail by turns, and was very handy when working out how to describe the knots above.

In this way, we all express our personalities through a tiny piece of cloth. Somehow I don't think any of us would have got a job at Miss Miller's *Vogue* . . .

(For more information, call CanTeen on 1800 639 614 or visit www. canteen.com.au)

Turning Japanese

I'm having a Japanese moment. Not as in Comme, or Issey, or Yohji (the world's sexiest man, but that's another story), or even Akira, or Tetsuya. But Japanese as in *The Pillow Book* of Sei Shonagon. I know the whole *Pillow Book* groove was really some time ago, but I just happen to have read several books in a row with a Japanese theme, and that Shonagon thing is very infectious. You start thinking in her style. Or trying to. Let me give you some examples of things she wrote in the Imperial Court a thousand years ago:

> Things That Give a Pathetic Impression: the voice of
> someone who blows his nose while he is speaking. The
> expression of a woman plucking her eyebrows.
> Unsuitable Things: a woman with ugly hair wearing a robe
> of white damask.

Elegant Things: a white coat worn over a violet waistcoat.
A rosary of rock crystal.
Squalid Things: the back of a piece of embroidery. The
inside of a cat's ear.

Isn't that all heaven? Sei Shonagon's style statements are as
self-confident and outrageous as Diana Vreeland's, and
everything she wrote – in the tenth century AD – is still
fantastically relevant in the twenty-first century. Which
got me thinking, what would she be writing now? Perhaps
it might be something like this:

Things That Are Oddly Disturbing: a man who wears a
suit and has his hair tied back in a ponytail. A mobile
phone attached to a belt. Rings that are worn on the
forefinger. Hair that is longer than a certain length. All-
white outfits. The look and sound of false nails on a
computer keyboard.

Things That Always Delight: a folded cotton T-shirt that
has not yet been worn. The smell of a shirt that has been
worn for one day by a man you love. The small horizontal
crease that appears above the upper lip of some people
when they smile broadly. A child aged about two-and-a-
half with very pink cheeks, who is wearing a hat.

Things That Are Highly Irritating: when one is trying
on a garment and a salesperson comes into the changing
room. The garment is half on and half off. One's face is red.

The salesperson smiles. This is most annoying and humiliating. Or when the shoe one has been searching for is found, but not in the right size. A very expensive face cream which brings out red splotches on the cheeks.

Things That Are Always Unappealing: the thought of wearing pantyhose underneath trousers. Pantyhose worn with open shoes. An outfit that is too obviously new. A leather suit. The sight of acid-washed jeans worn with a brown belt.

Things That Are Strangely Attractive: men whose legs are slightly bandy. Women whose teeth are not quite perfect. A scar in a young man's eyebrow. A short-sleeved T-shirt worn over a long-sleeved T-shirt. Strong male bodies that have gone slightly to seed.

Sometimes the most unattractive person has a beautiful smile which makes you forget their less fortunate qualities. This induces a warm feeling.

Making excuses

How do you justify your love? My mother used to say, 'I can always wear it for gardening' whenever she had bought some dubious garment on a whim. Now she says, 'I have to buy things that are comfortable.' I remember her once coming home with a pair of high-heeled sandals in yellow polka dot fabric. 'They are a bit loud,' she said that time. 'But I'm sick of being matronly.' There was no arguing with it.

My friend Giovanna has turned shopping justification into an art form. We can hardly wait for her to buy something else she doesn't need, so we can hear what she comes up with to make it seem that she would have been foolish, rude or even insane not to have bought it.

Just before she went off to live in London, when she was saving every cent she could – in case she wants to have the odd cup of coffee while she's there – she came to Sydney on a farewell trip and turned up to meet me clutching a Marcs carrier bag.

'It was on sale . . .' she started, showing me a nice little jumper.

'It was reduced by 70 per cent and I thought I should be waving the flag for Australian designers in London . . .'

Here she demonstrates two advanced techniques of profligacy justification – the Unmissable Bargain tactic and the altruistic it-would-have-been-churlish-not-to manoeuvre. Two in the one sentence. Brilliant. The chick is a master.

One method I have always found particularly useful is the My Difficult Body routine. This is a sound justification for buying something expensive in several colours, and consists simply of an explanatory sentence along the lines of, 'Well, it's so difficult for me to find shoes for my wide feet, I thought I had better get three pairs.'

This works equally well for big boobs, short waists, fat tummies, stumpy legs, skinny butts, long slippery feet, ski-slope shoulders, butcher's arms, carthorse ankles, barge arses and any other figure flaw you are prepared to lay public claim to.

I 'needed' it is another good one. I needed some new evening wear. I needed something bright for summer. I needed some more clothes that weren't black. I needed something that said This Season. I needed another pair of black jersey trousers just like the other three pairs. I needed to waste $100 on a hat. I needed another pair of shoes I can't walk in. I needed a good bloody talking to, that's what I needed.

A particular favourite of mine in this group is 'I needed something to wear to work.' Can you see how cunning that is? Your work ethic made you do it.

A new one I am hoping to work up in this department is 'It's tax deductible', because I reckon I really deserve some recompense in that department. Do you know that even though I have to go to fashion shows and fashion parties as part of my work, none of my clothes are tax deductible? Workmen who have to buy steel toecap boots and overalls to protect them from injury can claim them against tax, but fashionistas who have to buy Prada bags and Jil Sander suits to protect them from sniggery can't.

It's outrageous. But I'm hoping that the Giorgio Armani shirt I bought to wear promoting my book and have worn on four TV shows will be. And it was the most amazing bargain as well. I think the tax department should reward me for being a canny shopper.

The golden fleece

Will polar fleeces one day be considered quaint? I had that thought on the Paris Métro, when I looked at the arm of the woman clinging onto the pole next to me and saw that she was wearing a red polar fleece jacket.

Despite numerous visits for work I am still starry-eyed enough about the French capital to find a ride on the Métro thrilling, and seeing polar fleeces there – on a Frenchwoman (although probably not a Parisienne, in truth) – made me realise just how ubiquitous the fabric has become.

When I got over to England a couple of weeks later, my mother was wearing a polar fleece pants and gilet outfit around the house – so soft, so warm, so cosy – and while I was there, a smart chocolate brown polar fleece throw rug arrived in the post.

From being a slightly mad professor invention (isn't it made from old plastic bottles or something?) worn only by Arctic explorers and white-water rafters, the polar fleece has become the universal fabric of the epoch. The stuff that we all wear. It's like jeans — everybody has at least one polar fleece item. (I have three: a grey hooded sweat top object, a red zip-front jacket object and a red ski hat object.)

And that was what made me wonder what kind of place polar fleeces would take in history, because while it seems like the most banal unfashion fabric now, anything that has been so universally adopted will not be forgotten.

With its environmentally aware fabrication, technological pragmatism (unbelievably light and warm — and water repellent), it will come to be associated very particularly with this era and will therefore become quaint, because time seems to invest everything with charm. Even tea towels.

For Christmas last year two of my best (and most aesthetically developed) girlfriends gave me tea towels. Not just any old tea towels, but old ones, found in French markets, with my initials serendipitously embroidered on them. One of them is about eighty years old, the other could be from 1800, or even earlier. You can tell by the irregularities in the fabric that the unbleached linen has been handwoven and the initials are rendered in a red cross stitch, redolent of early American colonial samplers.

As you can imagine, I was thrilled with my tea towels

and the really old one has the special status of being the bathroom hand towel I never actually use – it's just there to look beautiful and impress friends. I wouldn't dream of using either of them to dry dishes.

But I wonder what the women who embroidered those tea towels so long ago would think of their workaday wash cloths being treated as antique treasures. They'd probably think I was nuts. Just as my mother shuddered in horror when she saw I had an old painted meat safe in my sitting room as a fabulous 'distressed' cabinet. To her, it was such a reminder of the meat surrounded by a cloud of flies from the days before there was a fridge in every home, she could hardly bear to look at it. Whereas for me, brought up in the whitegoods-for-all 1960s, it is an object of great charm and character.

I can only assume that in years to come, people will look back on polar fleece garments with a winsome smile. Certainly Oscar-winning costume designers of the twenty-second century will have to learn to re-create the exact pilling effects for films set in the late twentieth century, just as Catherine Martin must have learned to be a whiz with a can-can knicker for *Moulin Rouge*.

It's hard to imagine a future style maven chancing upon my old grey polar fleece sweat top with a shriek of discovery in a market in the year 2100, but it could happen.

Acknowledgements

This book would not have been possible without the following wonderful women. Fenella Souter. Jane Wheatley. Susan Skelly. Cindy McDonald. Roz Gatwood. Helen Long. Sally Treffry. Lucy Tumanow-West. Deborah Cooke. Lenny Ann Low. Julie Gibbs. Sophie Ambrose. Debra Billson. Fiona Inglis. Miuccia Prada. The Fendi sisters. Coco Chanel.